Soulful
BRANDING

Unlock the Hidden Energy in
Your Company and Your Brand

*by Jerome Conlon,
Moses Ma &
Langdon Morris*

Library of Congress Cataloging-in-Publication Data
Conlon, Jerome
Soulful Branding a
p. cm
ISBN 978-1515114413
I. Business - Non-fiction. I. Title.

This is a pre-publication sample
Published in the United States

For more information:
(503) 313-8488 USA
jeromeconlon@gmail.com
www.futurelabconsulting.com

For Edward, Josephine &Karen

You illuminate a brighter way and a better path. Your friendship, courage and love are the foundations of this story.

– Jerome

For Qian

Every poem, song or book I write... is for you.

– Moses

For Elizabeth, McKenna & Keegan

Who teach me daily about the amazing power of love, and of the soul.

– Langdon

Praise for This Book

"This MUST READ book, Soulful Branding, takes you on an inspirational journey to the foundations of what great brands do. Far too many brands are lifeless trademarks, managed only by the numbers and emotionally disconnected from their consumers. Instead, successful marketers must build brands that resonate deeply with their audiences. In these pages you will find a practical yet thought-provoking guide to transformational brand management - how to create an iconic brand that radiates success and encourages customers to connect soulfully. I recommend it highly!"

— Jack Canfield, Creator of the Chicken Soup for the Soul brand and winner of The World's Best Brands "Brand Laureate Signature Award"

'Rebellion is what lies at the heart of innovation.' Soulful Branding is a book which continually prods its readers to reject the status quo and think differently about how to evoke consumers to connect emotionally with their brand and products. Executives in any discipline will benefit greatly by, not just reading, but absorbing the messages in this book.

— Tom Clarke, President of Innovation, Nike, Inc.

"In today's new business environment if your brand does not have a soul... it's dead! Soulful Branding is visionary and lays out the future of branding for any business that plans to be relevant".

— Deepak Chopra, Author, Soul of Leadership

'Soulful Branding' is a deep dive into the psyche and gestalt of understanding who we are as unique makers, story tellers and sellers. In short, this book is a must read for anybody who wants to excel in business. Of course, I'm a designer, so what the heck do I know about Branding?'

– Tinker Hatfield, Senior VP Design Nike, Inc.

"Brands are essentially human constructs. They are not made of rubber, metal, plastic or silicon. Humans design them, guard them, sell them and cripple them by their actions. A company that honors the human spirit and shares its values the way Nike, Apple or Starbucks did in their defining moments can create much deeper customer and employee relationships. They operate on a much higher, and more profitable level. This book is about the magic that resides beyond the logic, and that powerful swirl of emotional connectivity most companies fail to recognize, much less deliver. Great brands don't just cushion our feet, keep us warm or get us from point A to point B. They also touch our souls along the way. Few people have more experience in this rarified level of business alchemy than Jerome Conlon.

– Scott Bedbury, Author 'It's A New Brand World', Former Global Advertising Director, Nike and Chief Marketing Officer of Starbucks.

"The ethos Soulful Branding rests on is a challenge to taking the easy path, to branding by bullet point. Soulful Branding embraces the intangibles, the energy, life and wonder winding like cosmic worm-holes through the popular culture of our time. Thank you for this."

– Arnie Jacobson, Principle & Founder of the Qualitative Research Centre

Jerome Conlon is one of the most astute, experienced and creative brand theorists around. He has brought all his considerable talents to Soulful Branding, a truly unique take on branding and brand development. Insightful and engaging, Soulful Branding provides rare glimpses into what makes strong brands really tick in both theory and practice. It will undoubtedly strike a chord and fundamentally change how you think about branding. Soulful Branding will help you build better brands.

– Kevin Lane Keller, E.B. Osborn Professor of Marketing, Tuck School of Business at Dartmouth College, Author, Strategic Brand Management (4th ed.) and Co-Author (with Philip Kotler) of Marketing Management (15th ed.)

"The future of the music industry is in turning performing artists and groups into soulful, iconic brands. To achieve this end the projection of the right sound, look, meaning and persona is key. It's fascinating to see that many of the intangibles responsible for success in the performing arts are being employed in corporate and product brand planning. Soulful Branding provides a glimpse into the serious and entertaining side of brand character development"

— Jim Caparro, CEO & Founder Entertainment Distribution Company, Chairman & CEO of Warner Elektra Atlantic at Warner Music Group Chairman & CEO of The Island Def Jam Music Group at Universal Music Group, President & CEO Polygram Group Distribution at Polygram, Inc.

"Every once in awhile a new book arrives that wakes us up and inspires us to think differently. Soulful Branding is just such a book and a welcome contribution to the business of brand building. We are at a crossroads in modern branding practices, with too many marketers making branding a mechanical exercise, devoid of personality or depth, and too many companies lacking any sense of authenticity. Jerome Conlon offers truly refreshing and thought-provoking ideas for building brands, reminding us that we have a responsibility to not just have our brands make money, but make meaning."

— John A. Davis, Dean, Global MBA and MGB, Professor of Marketing, S P Jain School of Global Management, Dubai-Singapore-Sydney

"Soulful Branding's unique point of view holds the keys for any Corporation's message or products to live and have consumer value in the shifting marketplace. Without this deep understanding, Branders and marketers will live in complete darkness."

— Tyrone Davis, CEO / Chairman, Urbintra Entertainment Media Corporation.

"A great read for those who want to push the conventional boundaries and tap deeper into the true triggers of brand impact, attraction and loyalty. You are challenged to deepen your perspective on the importance of branding and how it affects outcomes over time. Soulful branding draws some powerful metaphoric parallels that are often overlooked. This is a unique and fresh perspective that is long overdue and worth the read!"

— Darrel Branch, CEO The Branch Out Group, Former head of Global Customer and Brand Marketing, The Coca Cola Company and National Sales Executive Revlon and Procter & Gamble

"Soulful Branding is a well crafted combination of business acumen mixed with psychology, mythology, and detective work. Conlon and Ma have put together a compelling argument for reframing our concept of who we are and what we represent as a company and as individuals. We are all projections of our perception, and getting to the heart of the matter illumines the greater potential we have to be harbingers of change and service for worthwhile outcomes and greater respect for all. Soulful Branding offers a model with examples that replace outworn modes of management and identity with open concepts that transform the way we do business and life! This book can be a game changer for any enterprise and is worth using to chart a course for meaningful success!"

– Kathleen Jacoby, Author, Vision of the Grail

"Soulful Branding fills a void in the world of branding, in a profound way."

– Madonna White, Entrepreneur, CEO Got Cheers

"Soulful Branding is like a three dimensional chessboard that peers into branding strategies that only few can see. This should be a manual for anyone trying to tap into the psyche of the artist and their brand. Although no one can predict the next big thing – Soulful Branding comes close to laying out the roadmap."

– Evan Forster, CEO The Huddle Campus & The Dream School

"The relationship between companies and consumers is crucial, but business books don't often tackle the softer side of this reality. 'Soulful Branding' does explicitly, exposing the secrets of brands' intangible assets with examples from some of the most recognizable, relevant and valuable companies we engage with today. "

– Ryan Fiorentino, Strategist, Ziba Design

Contents

Contents

Appendices

Foreword

"So, what song does your brand sing?" asked Jerome Conlon on the day we met. It wasn't the question that I had been expecting.

As it turned out, though, it was exactly the right question. I had engaged Jerome as a consultant, hoping he could help my company give one of our aging brands a facelift, infuse it with a more contemporary and appealing personality. His response was that we were asking the wrong question, and looking for answers in the wrong place. You can't fix a brand by changing its wardrobe, he explained. Consumers will know you're faking it, and they will turn away.

During the next few days Jerome took my team on a deep dive into our "brand truths" to strip the brand down before we dressed it up, to find its heart, and to allow the heart to tell its story. It was a transformative exercise, not just for the brand, but for everyone who participated.

And for Jerome and me, it was the start of a beautiful friendship.

Since then we have enjoyed many branding collaborations, most of them successful. In these jam sessions we play odd couple roles; Jerome is the poet-storyteller, and I'm the empiricist-engineer. The combination has proven remarkably productive, and proves the point about differences of perspective adding IQ points.

Many years later, Jerome and I were working on re-branding a consumer tech company, one with an exceptional product line but with an image as exhilarating as a speed bump. The company's leadership team shared deep and privately held spiritual beliefs, but in public they were uncomfortable talking about anything other than their technology. The branding brainstorm session seemed log-jammed, when suddenly Jerome began humming a song. Immediately, everyone in the room broke out in smiles, because it just felt right. That song became the anchor of a remarkable branding campaign, and it tested off the charts.

It worked because you just couldn't listen to that song without feeling your spirits soar, without feeling optimistic despite all the troubles in the world. And that was precisely the message that the company's leadership wanted to deliver; it was Jerome who found the right voice.

By what logic did Jerome arrive at the musical key to this branding puzzle? Certainly not by a logic informed only by reductive analysis. Instead, he tuned in to the energy field surrounding the company and its products, and there he found music that resonated with it. The key might have been some other subjective cue—a work of art, a line from a poem, a folk allegory. What mattered was the emotional resonance, the force that trumps all others.

I learned from Jerome to think of the character of the brands I managed like I thought of the character traits of my own children. Should they aspire to be glib, trendy, and aggressive? Or wise, caring, and delightful? Pretty obvious when the question is posed that way, but it so rarely is. And so we see example after example of brands beating their chests and hurling insults at their competition when they should be opening their hearts to the people they desire to serve.

At first, however, I was taken aback when Jerome told me that our job is to enable brands to give and receive love with their fans. Over the years that we have worked together, I have learned just how astonishingly right he is.

On a number of occasions I have watched as Jerome transformed the way seasoned marketing professionals think about branding. The marketers begin the day believing that brands are fortresses built from USPs, creative cleverness, and competitive positioning, but in the end they realize that brands are primarily temples built from core beliefs, values and storytelling.

Soulful Branding is Jerome's masterwork, his magnum opus. With his consulting partners and co-authors Moses Ma and Langdon Morris he has created a bible (with a bit of Kama Sutra thrown in) for building brands that are worthy of being loved by their consumers. But the creation of Soulful Branding was no easy task. The first draft was more like an unabridged encyclopedia than a business book, weighing in at well over 1,000 pages. Happily, Moses and Langdon helped Jerome concentrate and distill his wisdom into the more manageable 200 pages that you're reading now.

And while most business books consist of just one or two good ideas that could be fully expressed in a few pages, but instead are inflated to meet a publisher's required minimum page count of 125+, that's definitely not the case with Soulful Branding. This is a book to be sipped, savored, and reflected upon. Because it won't just change the way you approach branding. It will change the way you see almost everything – your job, your life, and even your relations with others – and the brands you manage as well.

For example, you'll learn that the overwhelmingly decisive factors in almost all human decisions are instincts, emotions, and subconsciously received signals. The book describes "depth campaigns," such as those by Apple Nike, where the advertising showed little or no actual product because rather than talking about products, their advertising tells stories that illuminate the companies' compelling values and deeply held beliefs.

Obviously, this approach has resonated with consumers, and it has served Apple's and Nike's shareholders equally well.

In the early 1990s, about the time I first met Jerome, we worked together on a branding campaign for Sega of America. For the first time in video game advertising history, game players were portrayed as the rebellious, irreverent, in-your-face teenage boys that they really are. These ads irritated adults and mortified the competition, but video gamers, voting for the console company that deserved their dollars, deeply rewarded Sega by more than tripling our market share in less than a year.

And what's just as remarkable as the branding success stories, including the Sega story, that are related in Soulful Branding is how infrequently such successes occur. This book reveals all the tricks of trade, so why are they employed so rarely? Why do the vast majority of branding campaigns leave consumers cold, bored, or irritated? What are these brand management teams thinking? Apparently they haven't yet read this book, but it's not too late.

If they're only thinking "business is war," they're going to have a hard time getting their heads around "branding is love," but's that's precisely the compelling message delivered in this book by Jerome, Moses and Langdon.

For all the out-of-touch brand managers you know, Soulful Branding may be just the thing to increase their Branding IQ and EQ by those fabled 80 extra points, giving them a transformative change of perspective. Soulful Branding is by far the 21st century's best guide to branding, and I hope you find it as insightful as I have.

Doug Glen
Hong Kong
February 2015

Doug is former Chief Strategy Officer of Mattel Toys, Chief Executive of Imagi Studios, General Manager of LucasArts Entertainment, and Group Vice President of Sega of America.

Preface

Soulful Branding presents a new, 21st Century brand management framework, along with the tools and processes that will help you to develop more powerful, more inspiring, and more successful brands by unlocking and elevating the hidden energies inside your company and its brand field.

Our thesis, expressed here with numerous examples of real world discoveries inside some of the world's most iconic brands, is that those that have attained the highly desirable state of brand soulfulness have done so with great intent and distinctive skill, and they show us that when the body, mind and spirit of a company and its brands are fully aligned and working together in harmony, it creates a soulful brand character that enables far greater success than can be achieved any other way.

To set the stage, let's examine some basic concepts. I'll start with the concept of the soul since the word 'soulful' is a foundational concept of this book. The soul I refer to doesn't pertain to objects of religious belief, nor to concepts related to immortality, but rather one we're all capable of sensing as we make our way in life. We perceive it with our feelings and intuition as a quality of experience that arises when we engage profoundly with others, or when we perceive something sublime, such as beauty, truth, and goodness.

Soul-minded writers and thinkers over the centuries have emphasized common recurring themes reminding us that this soul is connected with intimacy, personal attachments, love, places where love and meaning flourish such as warm cafes, soothing gardens, and uplifting community celebrations, where heightened levels of relatedness and a transcendent spirit is present.

Soulfulness is connected with genuineness and depth of character, with great meals lovingly prepared and shared, with fulfilling conversations, authentic friends, and experiences that remain long in the memory and profoundly touch the heart.

Soulfulness also enhances the character of music and indeed all the arts as a force that resonates through people who radiate warmth, wisdom, regard, respect and love. In this sense it relates to the total personality and it speaks simultaneously to both our conscious and subconscious senses of knowing.

This matters so much because we're painfully aware that the vast majority of brands in today's marketplace have vastly simplified identities. Most are positioned around logical appeals to physical needs or intellectual concepts, and most marketing activities are focused on promoting only tangible benefits simply because this is the easiest and most obvious thing to do. Tangibles appeal to the five senses, reflecting the traditional marketing and brand development approach that is firmly grounded in pragmatism.

And marketers believe that pragmatist customers want sensible value, not sophisticated or extreme performance or design. While this market segment may constitute as much as 50% of the total market in some categories, this is decidedly not the segment that leads in the adoption of the most distinguished and differentiated products, nor the ones at the higher end, and because it's usually at the higher end of the price, value, and quality spectrum that brand thought and image leadership is determined, the pragmatist approach means by definition settling for second place.

In Soulful Branding we aim high and also deep, so we consider multiple perspectives and dimensions that enable and support the best brands. For example, consider the profound significance of our senses. Did you know that we have far more than five? While many of us were taught that the human body has five senses, sight, hearing, touch, taste, and smell, neurologists now identify as many as twenty-one. (Just for reference, the commonly held definition of a "sense" is "any system that consists of a group of sensory cell types that respond to a specific physical phenomenon, and that corresponds to a particular group of regions within the brain where the signals are received and interpreted.")

According to this definition, modern scientists have proposed additional senses: thermoception, our capacity to sense heat and cold, proprioception, the ability to tell where your body parts are relative to other body parts (which is one of the factors that police officers test when they pull over a suspected drunk driver), nociception, our ability to sense pain, and magnetoception, some people's ability to detect magnetic fields.

Ancient Egyptians believed that humans had even more, as many as 330 senses. For example, they believed that we sense a wide array of meanings from different vocal tones. An urgent command, for instance, is delivered with a completely different intonation from a casual question, while the sensation of a whisper is very different from that of a shout, so every spoken or written word that is received and interpreted provides people with a unique sensation that is received and interpreted by the brain.

In *Soulful Branding* we make observations and draw conclusions about how people use this expanded range of sensing and sensitivity to determine how they feel about brands. And from our career experiences we know that companies that learn to work with this broader palette of tools and hidden energies can also learn to create value in new ways.

This is important information for brand planners because there are intense forces of commodification at work in the marketplace. Competition is global, and since the world-wide-web has made it so easy for consumers to compare prices, branding strategy has to be about using factors other than price to create meaningful differences that influence purchase decisions. This understanding has forced leading brand managers to work intensely to achieve differentiation through factors including product design, experience design, retail design, brand communications, brand image, and brand character, and to strive to express soulfulness in each of these dimensions. These are all topics that we will explore in depth throughout this book.

Further, in the brand-planning world that we come from, not all projects are created equal. Costs or revenues are not by themselves the only major determining factors, because intelligent brand initiatives are designed to create "integrated value," which is how some brands separate from the mass and move into leadership positions within their categories.

And by focusing on integrated value, brand meaning can be rejuvenated and redefined over time; given the changing world we live in, this is not only an option, but often a necessity. Projection techniques in research can be used to explore the gap between a current state and a more ideal state, not just in products, but in how your brand is perceived and regarded. This work can lower barriers to future sales and it can expand the relevance and resonance of your products to wider circles of consumers. You'll find examples throughout this book of how leading brands have used this knowledge to move forward.

We do this while remembering that soulful branding cannot replace the fundamentals related to the tangible benefits of products, the need for crisp operations, or the importance of sales execution. The principles of soulfulness can and indeed must be integrated with traditional disciplines and values, and it's entirely logical to construct business and brand initiatives that meet multiple goals simultaneously.

Character Development and Branding

Another word we use throughout the book is "character," particularly as it relates to brands and branding. What do we mean by this? Character in a person or in a brand is the aggregate of features, traits and behaviors that form the individual's nature or personality. In the theatre, characters represent iconic personality types by emphasizing distinctive traits such as language, mannerisms, physical makeup, motives, and beliefs. Storytellers know that the characters they create need to have character as well as coherence, they need to add up and behave consistently, even when they can also present twists and surprises, just as people do.

Developing brand character has many things in common with screenwriting, and the attempt to develop relatable characters for film and TV. Relatable characters are drawn up as sympathetic heroes on a mission to achieve worthy goals. They're often created as original, attractive, intelligent and provocative, and definitely not corny, cliché, predictable or superficial. They have a definite point of view and a convincing way of getting it across. Many also have an underlying sense of humor and irony, which help to make it easy for people to relate to them. They're frequently involved in acts of moral integrity to resolve some sort of problem or dilemma, and they speak in a distinctive voice that resonates. As their story develops, the complexity of their character emerges, often showing surprising depth. Above all, relatable characters that become hits get people talking about them.

Seasoned screenwriters know these qualities can be enhanced by their choice of story. They know that audiences need to find themselves in the story, and develop a rooting interest for the characters.

Hence, screenwriters often start by researching the character back-story. They get to know their character's history, values and development context so they have a strong sense of what's consistent for their character to do and say.

This is relevant to us because there are important parallels between brand development and hit show character development, and my career path from Nike, to Starbucks, to NBC has allowed me to reflect on these parallels. In fact, a lot of my Soulful Branding experiences come as a result of working to identify and express authentic character traits that unfold over the arc of a brand's story.

To begin exploring this question in a more personal way, let's try a simple thought experiment. You can try this alone, but it works even better doing it together with a few others.

First, name three brands that you have personally encountered that you feel expressed interesting character traits, and which led you to have affinity for the brand itself. Why did you select these three brands out of the thousands of possibilities?

Next, ask yourself why you bought each of these brands the very first time? The first answer you give is generally not the real answer, and if we were in a small group and I was asking why over and over again, we'd first hear the obvious, tangible reasons. In persisting the intangible impressions may start to surface. These include the emotional benefits, such as how it felt to use the brand under ideal circumstances.

We might also identify brand character traits you admire. If you drive a BMW, for example, do you feel that it really is the "ultimate driving machine?" Is it a brand for serious, high-performance aficionados? If this brand were a person, what kind of person would it be? Would it really be a fit, athletic, aggressive German male?

We might examine if the brand has been an effective advocate, championing a worthy cause? At Starbucks we were striving to produce extraordinary coffee experiences, stamp out badly brewed coffee, take genuine care of our employees, and create an ethical and sustainable global coffee supply, all at the same time. Have we succeeded?

Brands are sponges for content and personal experiences in this way, and they absorb connotations and associations on a constant basis.

These qualities that brands absorb they then project, and this has tremendous impact on the quality of a person's perception, experiences and associations with a brand as well as the reputation and regard that they attribute to it. Brands with the strongest likeability and those that evoke feelings of trust, respect, esteem and affinity rank at the top of the list for the most discerning consumers in most categories. These strong brands also command the highest margins, attract and retain the best talent, and tend to be more resilient in times of adversity.

I've asked these brand projection and personification questions hundreds of times with people around the world. I've always found that the personification exercise that asks, if the brand were a person, what kind of person would it be, reveals very insightful image associations, issues and opportunities for brands. This exercise also reveals something important about the character traits people really admire and identify with, as well as what people notice and respond to energetically. I've discovered that it's not just the tangible products that matter most in forming reputation, relationships and preferences. Many intangibles lead to the strongest brand relationships, and there are hundreds of impressions that can serve as attractors or irritants in the minds of consumers.

My Own Soulful Branding Journey

My understanding of the nature of brands and brand development started in my high school years of running track and continued through college as I ran competitive road races and marathons, wearing out countless pairs of running shoes along the way. Constantly looking for better shoes in performance and aesthetics, I read magazines and books on running. Eventually I began noticing quirky but thoughtful ads from a small running shoe company in Beaverton, Oregon called Nike. These early Nike magazine print ads spoke directly to committed runners like myself, less so about the technical specs of their shoes than the soulful experience embedded deep within our sport. "The race is its own reward," was one ad tagline that stood out. And another: "There is no finish line."

I identified with these messages, and it was also the spirit behind the messages that intrigued me. And this led me, while still in college, to target Nike as a most desirable place for me to work. It took me two years of knocking on their door, but eventually my persistence paid off when I met someone who knew someone who worked there, and I pressed my connection for an information interview.

So I met with Tony Gault, head of IT systems in March of 1982. In preparation I read everything I could get my hands on about the company, a stack of research about two feet thick. Tony opened by asking me, "So what do you know about Nike?" and man was I prepared for that question!

I shared what I knew about the history, characters, ideals and products behind Nike, about how Bill Bowerman was connected to the start of the running movement in the US, and I spoke of the company's great growth potential as a brand. Tony stopped me after about ten minutes and mentioned that I knew more about the company than many of the people who worked there. "I have this idea for a new job that I think you'd be perfect for. Are you interested?"

A week later I interviewed with Nike's COO Del Hayes for a position called "Information Center Manager." He sized me up and then provoked me with this line: "I suppose you're one of them god-damned runners." Without missing a beat I replied, "Well, running is a vice I have, but I try not to push it off on people who aren't ready for it."

And so I entered deep inside the world of Nike for a fourteen-year run, the beginning of a transformational experience in my understanding of what is possible in the world of soulful branding.

But my brand planning experience at Nike didn't begin until 1986, as I held the Information Center job for two years, then moved into finance for the next two. This was a fit for me since my college degrees were in accounting, economics, and business, but I also had a strong connection with the arts. And it is the marriage of the arts – design, architecture, literature, advertising, entertainment, and storytelling – with numbers and with planning that sums up my career path.

My family origin and childhood also had a deep influence on my career path and educational development. I was born in England of British parents who immigrated to the United States when I was three years old. I spoke with an English accent, and other children made fun of me; this introduced me to various dynamics of perspectives and values, which later proved to be very helpful in doing brand development work.

As I was turning six, my father completely lost his eyesight. He had been diagnosed with a degenerative eye disease in his late teens, and in college trained at the only school in the world that taught blind or partially sighted people to become physical therapists. He ran a very successful practice at a local hospital for thirty years after he went blind.

His blindness made me keenly aware of the gift of sight. I felt sad for my father, whom I thought had been dealt a terrible blow in life. In spite of it, he maintained a cheery disposition. With a great sense of humor he was able to inspire people with physical disabilities to overcome them, as he had done.

I would learn years later from my father that there are different kinds of sight. Dreams and visions are another kind, and both my mother and father knew how to view life as a soul journey that has a far deeper purpose beyond surface appearances. Then, just a few years ago I was having dinner with my father on his eighty-fifth birthday, and I asked him, "Do you have any big regrets in your life? If you could do it over, would you do anything differently?" His response surprised me.

"I have no regrets," he said. "I wouldn't do anything differently. Going blind the way I did, I can now see, was the best thing that ever happened to me. Without going blind, I never would have found myself in the spiritual sense that I know myself today. Going blind opened up a new world for me that I didn't know existed. No, I wouldn't change a thing."

This was a revelation to me. I had thought ever since childhood that his affliction was something he coped with, but which had robbed him of something vital in his life. I had never considered that instead he was grateful for the blessings it had bestowed upon him.

From Nike to Starbucks

Throughout my years at Nike I found that the company's top managers readily supported innovation on many levels, not just in product design. The culture was ideally suited to challenging convention, and my efforts to introduce new tools, techniques and processes in brand planning were well supported.

The dilemma we faced in growing the company and coping with many challenges was that things were so complex and so fast moving that it was difficult to get an overview of the whole, and see the full picture. When we don't have that picture, or when we're not even questioning what part of the picture we're seeing, or not seeing, we often end up arguing strenuously from a partial view of "truth." The essence of this problem is one of limited perception, and it perfectly describes the central challenges in brand planning.

I've learned from decades of brand planning that most market and product categories are ripe for reinvention, but often the reason they're not reinvented is that the visioning skills and understanding of what's possible are lacking.

In 1996 I left Nike to join Starbucks and to support such a vision of what might be possible, and not surprisingly I found it to be quite a different culture from what I experienced in Oregon. Starbucks faced its own set of challenges, products, values and personality characteristics, and I was no longer dealing with athletes, but with all the issues surrounding the iconic coffee house, steeped in the aroma of history and its connection to art, literature, music, philosophy and even revolution.

My transition was made possible because Howard Schultz, Starbucks' founder and CEO, had a pressing concern about the development of the Starbucks brand; he wanted to know if the company was developing Starbucks in the right way, and he knew that if he didn't find the optimal way, one that also honored the unique role that coffee plays in our lives, that the business would fall far short of its growth potential.

Early-stage, high-growth brands like Starbucks present a massive challenge for brand planners. The company was opening more than one retail store a day, the fastest expansion in retail history. So when I was offered the VP Brand Planning position I wondered if my experience at Nike would translate into a different industry and organizational culture. I subsequently learned that some of the tools did translate well and some didn't, but the process of entering a new culture and adapting and testing tools and processes proved invaluable.

At Starbucks we faced a number of big challenges, and there were a lot of big questions that we needed to answer: Are the stores we're building going to pass the test of time? Is Starbucks following the QSR 'Quick Service Restaurant' model too closely? Are we losing touch with the soul of authentic coffee house culture? What is the optimal arrangement of design elements in coffee shops of different sizes? Who or what holds the emotional high ground in the specialty coffee category? Is there an ideal coffee shop? What is Starbucks' ultimate brand character and position? What are the big opportunities and threats on the growth path?

On my first day of the job, Starbucks Marketing VP Scott Bedbury, who had joined Starbucks from Nike and then lured me to follow him, gave me a simple assignment – he wanted me to read everything there was to read about the origins and history of coffee, and about Starbucks brand history and current position, and to let him know where the gaps were for the brand and for the category as a whole. Simple indeed! No wonder he called it "the big dig."

Brand backstory research like this allows a planning team to tease out the culture and values of the entire category, and then compare a brand to historic ideals and competitor positions.

We discovered, of course, that coffee is a soulful beverage that has played a unique role in the history of western civilization, helping to make society far more cultured and civil. Interestingly, one of the facts the research uncovered is that the Boston Tea Party, one of the foundational events of the American Revolution, also resulted in a cultural change in the colonies, as coffee soon became the young nation's preferred beverage.

We also discovered that Howard Schultz's big concern about building the brand was correct. Our big dig revealed that the Starbucks brand needed to develop its soulfulness by aligning more with 'ideal coffee house' and less with a Quick Service Restaurant model; we couldn't achieve the right positioning by imitating McDonald's.

The Qi of Soulful Branding

The essence of Soulful Branding equates metaphorically to the oriental concept of Qi or Chi (pronounced chee). In the West we sometimes call this the Life Force Energy that animates and supports us.

Advanced martial artists know that this energy can be felt, nurtured, blocked or moved around, and when it is nurtured and focused, Chi can increase strength and punching power many times over.

The legendary Bruce Lee mastered the power of Chi to deliver his famous one-inch punch, which sent his opponent flying across the room, and his book on the martial arts, *The Tao of Jeet Kune Do*, is a remarkable distillation of his remarkable philosophy. The core practice of Jeet Kune Do is to let go of form, to become formless and dynamic in every way while remaining fully grounded in form and classical theory and refined only by the filter of what really works.

This is what we aspire to in soulful branding. And one of our insights is that the hidden energy of Chi also exists as potential within businesses and brands. It can be used for far more positive things than beating up an opponent, for it can also express character in products and communication forms; the intent of this book is to explore how this can be achieved.

In Soulful Branding we propose that soulful character and deep, personal relationships are at the very center of how all great brands are developed. Our story will take you into recent discoveries in archeology, music, quantum physics and business to examine how the soul can bring hidden energy into view, and also help us understand how great brands can be defined and developed into powerful and positive global icons and landmarks along the journey to branding and operational excellence.

These shifts in perspective can have big implications for how your brand can achieve greater soulfulness and thus greater success in the rich and challenging years that lie ahead. My coauthors and I believe that the story of *Soulful Branding* can help you to achieve it!

Jerome Conlon
Portland, Oregon
March 2015

1 | *What is Soulful Branding?*

"The measure of mental health is the disposition to find good everywhere."
— Ralph Waldo Emerson

"A vision is not just a picture of what could be; it is an appeal to our better selves, a call to become something more."
— Rosabeth Moss Kanter

Everyone is experiencing the transition to a new, technology driven society, one that places ever-greater reliance on our connected and collective consciousness. As information and intelligence becomes more fully the domain of smartphones and machine learning, people in business are coming to realize that they must also place more value on the human qualities that cannot be automated, especially if they want to differentiate their brands.

The unique qualities of our inner lives still hold the essential keys to a better way of living, qualities such as connection, magnetic attraction, love, imagination, and inspired ideal forms and expressions, for these produce the greatest meaning and feeling. This inner human language is common to us all, and the leaders of successful brands are discovering that their importance only increases in this new, digitized world, for these are really the experiences that have the most influence on how we choose to live, how we engage with others, what we choose to do and not do, and also what we buy.

Because products and services are largely defined as "brands," it emerges that branding becomes central to the new world, and to its economy. Success in business absolutely requires a profound, focused, and skillful effort at brand creation, brand development and brand management.

In fact, a strong brand is vital to the success of every business. On average,

58% of the value of a Fortune 500 company is held in its intangibles, including intellectual property, goodwill, and of course the focus of our interest here, the strength and meaning of the brand.

The very best brands, those that are created, developed and managed with the most skill, are precisely the ones that evoke the most positive inner responses. The roles and magic moments that great brands can play in human life carry us beyond a simple physical identity and into the deeper world of brand character, persona, and meaning.

These great brands thrive on the basis of the stories and myths they express, and upon the feelings, connections, and emotions that they inspire. They carry shared and iconic meanings that carry identity value.

Hence, the linkage between human emotions, brands, and our inner selves is indelible, and it is the subject of this book. We are deeply interested in the power that you can deploy when you design brands that continually explore, embed, and describe new patterns of connection and meaning in higher-level harmonies with the thoughts, needs, beliefs, and aspirations of your customers.

By working intimately with great brands for more than three decades, we have learned that soulful qualities in leadership, branding and marketing can dramatically improve the strength and power of any brand, which of course brings with it a host of additional benefits including market share and sales growth, premium pricing and margins, customer and employee loyalty, and brand extensions. It also makes brands more resilient in times of adversity.

These highly desirable but largely intangible factors are the soul qualities of focus here, and our goal is to show you how to embody them in your brand to achieve something much higher, more enduring, and of far greater value, thereby forging stronger inter-personal relationships between your brand and the customers you are serving.

This is what we mean by "soulful branding."

2 | *The Soul of an Organization*

"Imagination is more important than knowledge. For knowledge is limited to all we now know and understand, while imagination embraces the entire world, and all there ever will be to know and understand.
— Albert Einstein

*We are the music-makers
And we are the dreamers of dreams
Wandering by lone sea-breakers
And sitting by desolate streams;
World-losers and world-forsakers,
On whom the pale moon gleams:
Yet we are the movers and shakers
Of the world forever, it seems.*
— Arthur O'Shaughnessy

We begin our exploration of soulful branding with the obvious but important recognition that any brand is an expression of the character, skills and imagination of the organization that creates it.

That organization is itself much more than its products and services, although it includes them; great organizations also have clear purposes, deep reasons for being, and they share those purposes, passions and motivations with their customers and all constituents in ways that are both overt and obvious, as well as subtle and subliminal. And of course they deliver great value into the marketplace, in the form of products and services that delight, surprise, astound, or just fully satisfy. Together, their products and their purposes largely define their identities, encompassing spirit, personality, character, intent and action, from the heights of vision to the critical realities of profitable, everyday operations.

Brands are the concise icons that represent everything that an organization is and does, and in this book we are very interested to explore how and why great brands embody the most profound and enduring soul qualities. This is not just an exercise in feeling good, though, for we can quantify the value of a brand in a fairly objective manner.

So how much is a strong, positive brand perception worth? The intangible value of a well-run company and its brand can be worth 55% to 80% of market capitalization, which for a large company can be an enormous sum. This equity is captured on the balance sheet by the term "goodwill," yet as significant as this value is surrounding the business, most companies entirely lack a clear process or a discrete set of tools to understand how to work with and leverage these hidden intangible values and equities. We will address that gap here.

As we noted above, a brand is the aggregate of everything that a company communicates about itself, its many voices and countless actions within the market, both the profound and soulful ones, along with the mundane and functional interactions with product and daily business operations. Great products, poorly branded or marketed will most likely fail to achieve their potential; great brands that produce mediocre products do not stay great for long.

Revealing the Soul of a Brand

Soulfulness itself is of course a deep and complex topic. It's not a one-dimensional quality, but one that encompasses a deep layering of relationships, sensibilities, values, design qualities, messaging, storytelling, and also a telling attribute of the culture of every organization.

A brand's soulfulness can be revealed through the artistic imagination as expressed in product design, in the quality and sincerity of service, through the power of well-crafted stories, and through the personalities or actions of admired and admirable characters, songs, poems, advertisements, and artistically completed ceremonies. It is also revealed in how people perceive that they are regarded.

Indeed, the fundamental concept of human regard is the broad and solid base of the mighty brand pyramid, because people both inside and outside of every company use their powerful senses to pick up the countless cues that express the real intentions and spirit behind every brand and company, and if regard for the people you serve is authentic, knowing and strong, your brand strength can reach to great heights.

In contrast to high levels of regard are the experiences and feelings of fear, distrust, doubt, disrespect, condescension and all the negative human qualities and emotions that are immediately obvious to customers and employees because we all immediately recognize tones, frequencies and vibrations on the subconscious level, well before the conscious brain has rationally processed the meaning of whatever was implied, said, or done. A negative tone on the human interactive field always shuts down the cooperative dynamic of sharing ideas and energy, and thereby diminishes a brand.

The opposite is certainly true, for demonstrating high regard for customers and employees expands the interactive energy field, which then expands the level of cooperative engagement and increases the range of what the players on the brand field can do and feel together. Co-creative energy feeds on shared passions that grow from this inter-personal dance, and organizations that harness this hidden power gain a significant long-term competitive advantage over those that don't.

Further, it is entirely possible for organizations to tap a form of loving regard as an innate organizing principle, as it requires only an enlightened consciousness and positive role modeling from business leaders for entire organizations to tap into this powerful source of engagement, motivation and creative imagination.

From the Brand Identity to the Interactive Field

In many organizations, the brand identity derives, as it should, from the aspirational or inspirational core values of a founder's personal passions, which leads to the creation of high-value products and services. Such a foundation can also lead to a positive work-life climate and values that become powerful sources of strength that can endure for years, decades, or longer.

Many companies, however, maintain only a functional brand identity, focusing on the mundane and largely ignoring these heart-centered human qualities and possibilities. Such brands may signify a firm's trademark, but they do not inspire familiarity, praise, admiration, or loyalty, for they appeal to physical needs, convenience or logic only, but not to deeper human emotional needs of the different constituencies they touch. Basic functional brands offer little soul depth and don't provide meaningful detailing of character, persona, or purpose beyond the functional.

This is the opposite of how brands with soul engage – they operate from a deep and resonant emotional core, often expressing an intimate understanding of the role that their products and services play in the lives of customers. They have character that is recognizable, appreciated and well defined. And to communicate the innate values of their organizations, these brands commonly employ branding strategies that evoke and celebrate the soulful qualities.

The public experiences these soul qualities when an event or impression brightens our mood or raises our spirits. Something resonates deeply within us, and we experience a quality of subtle energy, an evocative vibration or a nurturing sense of goodness.

Creative artists seek to embed these qualities in their works to evoke a feeling of inner life, to create worlds filled with purpose, passion, love, and light. And readers choose to engage in these worlds because they evoke moods, feelings, and intuitions, because they reveal new meanings or even inspire their own creativity, pushing forward our understanding about what is possible or desirable.

Greater success in business, then, often comes through brands, advertising, branded content and other experiences that are radiantly alive in exactly this way, filled with warmth of spirit, imbued with love and light, animated, resonant, and alive. Great brands project heart and soul energies that people intuitively and immediately respond to.

Hence, as a potter shapes clay, a composer shapes sounds, and a writer shapes words, the brand creator's medium encompasses all the factors that shape a brand's essence and identity, its messaging and most especially its meaning. Every communication, every product, every point of contact conveys deep literal and symbolic significance, and exists within a broader field of energy that is the sum total of all the messages and experiences. The net effect when all these elements have been arranged virtuously is one of affinity, respect, esteem, loyalty, high regard and even love.

And given recent developments in digital publishing for all kinds of branded content, it's now easier than ever to attach even more layered meaning and stories to a brand and the vibrant interactive field that surrounds it. But of course, a resonant brand message must be backed up with high quality experiences, products and services. When this occurs on a large scale, a brand can rise in the mind of the market to a position of eminence.

Thus, the art and science of guiding the creation and development of a brand's interactive field, and doing so in its entirety, is the essence of soulful branding.

A Different Perspective

Today, what we see more commonly in business development is a hyper-rational viewpoint on brand design and marketing, one dominated by spreadsheets, reams of market data, feedback metrics, and feasibility reports. Since

MBA programs primarily train future business managers in this hyper-rationalist point of view, it completely overpowers the soulful approach to soulful brand planning, which often lacks the deep insights and the mindset of a cultural advocate. The rationalist viewpoint, if left unchallenged, will smother the cultural insight and brand activism presented in this book. Authentic brand activism occurs in more fertile and nurturing company environments and withers in sterile, hyper-rational, management-by-logic-only environments. Soulful branding requires a greater perspective on life and living and a willingness to break rigid rules in order to risk moving people in more profound ways.

In the pursuit of a soulful brand, each instance, each touch point, can enhance the aggregate brand message that you aspire to create, or it can detract from it. Promotions, new advertisements, events, on-line campaigns, product packaging, and participation in the community are thus all part of the overall domain that we refer to as "the brand field."

Consequently, we recognize that everything employees say and do conveys deep meanings. This is why, for example, the Walt Disney Company spends so much time and effort to train the "cast" at Disneyland to create exactly the experiences that Walt Disney himself wanted each of his guests to receive. His attention to detail was notorious, and of course the remarkable results he achieved have defined Disneyland as one of the happiest places on earth.

The Disney brand today is instantly recognizable and globally appreciated, and it continues to endure and grow, reaching a worldwide audience of hundreds of millions of people through its theme parks, characters, movies, TV, print publications, and mobile media. What might be seen as fastidiousness by some can actually be interpreted as evidence of Walt's love for his company and its customers.

But this love of the company and its customers, and the attention to brand plus-ing, is how Disney unlocked the hidden energy and soul within his company.

Underlying these divergent expressions of the Disney brand was Disney's personal driving purpose, to become known as *"the world's premier storytelling entertainer"* with the simple aim of "making people happy," and he understood that each separate encounter was but one element among many in the creation of an overall brand reputation within the mind of the market.

Soul-filled, iconic brands engage with the world in a creative, inspiring and values-based way, as Disney surely does. Hence, when communications resonate with customers in this way, a brand conveys its soulful qualities into the lives of its customers, thereby enhancing those lives and also accruing still more value to the brand itself as it surrounds itself with an aura, a spirit, and a compelling way of being and feeling.

While rationalist branding starts out as a way to identify a product or a company in the marketplace, and then evolves into a means of beating the competition, it can evolve further into soulful territory, into an art form that is focused on cultivating the best qualities within both a company and its customers. A master of brand development senses and shapes the soulful energy field of a company and its brands, working and playing where science, mysticism, and management converge.

Art, Science, and Philosophy: The Soulful Organization

Because it is so pointedly focused on the most positive qualities, soulful branding is also a powerful way to develop an entire organization. This requires great attention to the personal mindset of both leaders and of employees, and done well it can evoke a remarkably positive organizational culture that can bring vitality to business and help develop companies and brands with living resonance, admirable character traits, and lovable personalities.

Hence, branding is not just a management science; it can also be practiced as an art and a philosophy that aspires to achieve the highest potential for brands, companies, employees, leaders, and customers. As a science, soulful branding teaches us to employ many different kinds of research approaches to grasp the realities of human relationships and a brand's interactive field, where human regard is present, where we sense and perceive the unarticulated needs and the unspoken aspirations of the people we're trying to win over and serve.

As an art and a philosophy, soulful branding is a profound medium of creative expression, a form likely to be perfected only after a long period of mindful effort, blending skills across many different disciplines.

As a problem-solving discipline, soulful branding works with the polar charges or qualities we all deal with in experiencing life. It entails Tai Chi'ing or moving the structures of energy around in product designs, advertising communication models or in retail environments.

The nuances of what we're talking about go beyond what's being taught in most schools today, and thus our goal for this book is to share the secrets of successful branding, secrets that have been discovered over many years of experimentation, practice and study, while sitting in the brand strategy hot seat of world class brands. Along the way we'll share many instances of deep learning – failures, that is – as well as some gratifying successes, all of which have helped us to understand and now articulate the principles and process of soulful branding. So let's venture together, now, into the hidden essence of branding, to discover its compelling inner soul.

3 | *Resonance*

"Music gives a soul to the universe
Wings to the mind,
Flight to the imagination,
A charm to sadness
Gaiety and life to everything,
It is the essence of order,
And leads to all that is good,
Just and beautiful,
Of which it is the invisible,
But never the less,
Dazzling, passionate and eternal form
– Plato

In southern Europe there are caves that were occupied and magnificently decorated by Paleolithic peoples some 20,000 years ago, and their many artistic wonders present a unique curiosity. In addition to their stunning visual arts, many of these caves have a surprising acoustic character, not only echoing sounds and voices, but also intensifying them.

If you visit them today you may notice that every sound you make lingers, reverberating from unexpected directions. This occurs due to the irregular shape of the walls, and in some places a cacophony of echoes ensues, each sound resonating long enough to merge with the next, thereby creating a continuous wall of acoustics that are rich, complex, and to the untrained ear, often disorienting. Whisper, hum, speak, or sing, and the sounds shout and sing back.

Archeologists have conducted experiments that reveal something even more remarkable. Moving slowly, and in total darkness along the narrow passages of caves at Arcy-sur-Cure in Burgundy and Le Portel near the Pyrenees, they use their voices like sonar to send out pulses of sound, and they receive resonant responses. At the precise point at which the soundscape shifts, they often discover paintings on the walls or ceilings, and where the tones resonate most profoundly there are often found the greatest concentrations of prehistoric paintings.

The first scientist to map in detail this stunning coincidence of the occurrence of resonance and prehistoric art was musicologist Legor Resnikoff. His detailed map of Arcy-sur-Cure reveals that nearly 80 per cent of the images in these caves were in locations of "living sound points," where the acoustics came to life with a determined poignancy.*

Similarly, if you go rock hunting in Horseshoe Canyon, Utah or in Hieroglyph Canyon, Arizona you'll find that those places with the greatest concentration of petroglyphs and pictures are exactly where echoes are strongest, or where sounds carry furthest.

The artists who worked in these special places 20 millennia ago obviously identified an invisible sense of spirit connected with echoes. Perhaps the compelling soundscapes indicated to them that spirits, unleashed through sound resonances, were nearby. Archeologists speculate that this connection led to the concentration of sacred art at these locations, as perhaps these special places were understood as gateways to the spirit realm where our ancestors could invoke the spirits for guidance, or bring greater meaning to life.

By sending out sounds and listening to their echoes and resonance, it's possible that cave artists experimented with sound not only to communicate with the spirit world, but also as a way to communicate with others, to share, bond, explore, and grow together.

In ancient times, and still today, music continues to occupy an extraordinary place in human culture, one that connects heaven and earth, as well as our subconscious minds with the physical world. Music is an outward expression of inner human resonance and deeply felt emotional energies.

Soulful Branding and music both connect with human essence. At the core of a soulful brand resides some facet of the spirit of humanity, and the creation of a soulful brand employs a similar process of sensing inner human resonances and then sending out sounds (often in the form of ideas or products), listening for their echoes, and creating distinct order and clarity from the seeming cacophony of sound (or feedback) that results.

Reflecting this sensibility, acclaimed musician and producer Quincy Jones

---

* *Noise – A Human History of Sound and Listening* by David Hendy, Harper Collins, 2013

once noted in a conversation with the author that he learned something important when he was working on the film *The Color Purple* with Steven Spielberg. "In the making of a movie, the most crucial phase is in scoring and laying down the soundtrack. This phase puts emotion into the film. This is crucial, because people go to the movies to be taken on some kind of emotional roller coaster ride." Sound indeed has that power in every setting, whether in movies, in caves, or in brands.

Harmony

Musician Mickey Hart expresses a similar sentiment with these words: "Many have described the essence of music as representing internal emotional states that cannot be put into words. Every musician knows this. The big question, the big mystery, is how to achieve this transfer of energy, how to translate your feelings into sounding movements and actions, and how these forms communicate so powerfully and precisely the original feelings. This process is, at least in part, what we mean by *Spirit into Sound*."*

In the physical world of sound waves, harmonic resonance is defined as the synchronization of sound frequencies. When two distinct sounds of the same frequency sympathetically resonate with each other, they interact across space. Thus, if there are two guitars in the same room and you pluck the string of one and let it vibrate for a few seconds, you may notice that the same string on the other instrument, which appeared to be untouched, is now vibrating. The vibration has traversed the space to make a literal, physical impact on the second instrument.

Harmonic resonance also describes what human beings feel in moments of profound aesthetic experience. Whether listening to a beautiful song or watching a beautiful sunset, extreme moments of sublime engagement when a person is apprehending truth, goodness or beauty, the inner harmonic resonance that results is capable of producing spine tingling sensations and mystical states of awareness.

A brand that we resonate with does the same thing, although typically to a lesser degree perhaps, by evoking a sympathetic vibration that slightly or even significantly alters our mood, and thus affects our inner self. We are not suggesting this as a metaphor, but as a literal reality – these are real vibrations that we feel and respond to.

In this way, it's important to recognize that a company can influence the meaning of its brand, but it doesn't really control it precisely because its value

---

* Mickey Hart, *Spirit Into Sound* – The Magic of Music, Grateful Dead Books, 1999, p21

is alive as something meaningful in the lives and minds of consumers.

That is, a brand is valuable because of the public's positive experience with the brand, and this positive experience is carried forward as a memory attached to the brand name and logo. Following this thought further, the brand logo is made up of all the experiences (positive, neutral and negative) that every consumer has ever had with it. Thus, a brand planner's vision about the future needs to be concerned not only with the nature of the brand's character and persona on the interactive brand field, but also with defining a consistent identity of touch points so the brand can be easily recognized in its essence and evolution.

These are complex requirements, and it's not surprising that this is difficult to do well, which explains why so many brands falter and seem to lose their way. Yet as the goal is to build brands that appeal effectively to the emotional state of consumers, as well as to their needs and aspirations, soulful branding is achieved when a brand triggers a positive emotional response in the consumer, that is, a desire that may not fully be rational even as it may be deeply felt.

Successful brands are emotionally resonant, and they have significant impact, because, as we have noted, consumers experience a strong and lasting attachment, a feeling of familiarity, bonding, companionship, and even love. Consequently, communications that speak to and evoke such positive inner experiences will resonate much more deeply.

But, this does not mean that brand communications must be loud to be noticed. They just need to be creatively interesting, rewarding to watch or hear, and evocative of the soul qualities that connect with the audience.

When they communicate in this soulful way, resonant brands actually alter space and thus access far more field energy than brands with little or no resonance or even worse, a dark and brooding presence. These principles of building meaningful relationships apply at the level of statesmanship as well.

Resonance

Have you ever been to a sporting event and noticed how the intensity of the crowd's involvement with the play on the field can vary from moment to moment? When a big play occurs that favors the home team, there's usually a dramatic rise in vibrational energy in the stadium, a roaring, rising wall of energy and sound. The roar is an outward, electric manifestation of an inward emotional state. Audiences thrive on that energy; in fact, many in attendance come for the emotional roller-coaster ride that a well-matched competitive game can produce.

So if the crowd you call your customers gets excited about your new product, or your new advertisement or viral video, then the intensity of positive word of mouth can also rise to a crescendo in the marketplace, just as the roar in a stadium rises at moments of high drama and exceptional performance.

Such resonance is also what the companies that advertise during the Super Bowl hope to achieve, but most Super Bowl ads fall flat because they communicate only in superficial dimensions, delivering only information, or attempting only to increase brand awareness.

Doing so, they dramatically under-utilize the power of the TV medium, which, along with internet video, is fully capable of generating greater brand interest and trial, of breaking through and saying something important, just as sounds inside of caves also once did. All brand communications have this potential, and they achieve it when the recipients find themselves inside of the story when their emotional chords are activated.

And this brings us to a critical point: a brand's symbolic meaning originates with its underlying purpose, and is expressed as a field vibration that radiates from the very core of a company. If a brand is to become iconic, to become a world-class energy that customers deeply identify with, then it must evoke the transcendent qualities of the soul. And to do that it has to express deep insight into its unique purpose in the world.

Such a deep brand purpose can be described as the intersection of three critical circles of influence. The first relates to an inherent or underlying issue or tension that creates a general or global problem which desperately requires resolving. The second relates to a core brand truth that expresses reasons for a brand's very existence. And the third connects the specific unmet consumer need in a way that the brand can legitimately address.

An example of this can be seen with Nike. Obesity and procrastination is a problem in American society for a

Figure 1. Brand Purpose

majority of the population. Nike's brand truth strives to capture and deliver 'authentic athletic performance' across thousands of sports and fitness products.

The consumer need revolves around the fact that everyone has a body and is therefore a potential athlete.

Nike's internal operational brand values are centered around "innovation, design and inspiration and how these three values can be continually interpreted anew to capture and deliver *'authentic athletic performance'* across thousands of sports and fitness products. The internal awareness of its core brand values and business purpose led to an inspirational brand campaign that has been in play off and on now in its advertising for more than 25 years. That campaign is the "Just Do It" campaign. The naming, claiming and alignment of your company mission, brand purpose, core values and brand positioning language is one of the most powerful sources of coherent wave amplification in brand positioning work.

When a company locates and codifies its brand purpose into a positioning platform and brand campaign as Nike did, it then becomes possible to emanate a level of soulfulness in communications that people crave, which then adds still more meaning and vitality to the brand. This is an example of a deep campaign, which we'll address in greater detail later in the book. It is a highly sought after virtuous circle, not easy to achieve, but absolutely worth striving for.

The Brand Conductor

Accomplishing this, of course, requires very attentive management, and the metaphor of a symphony illustrates the critical brand leadership role. A symphony orchestra usually has about ninety musicians, but if it's not well conducted then the music it plays isn't likely to sound very good, and may sound utterly awful. Every conductor's mission is therefore to interpret the composition while creating a compelling experience for the players and for the audience, while at the same time evoking the subtle tones, harmonies, melodies, and rhythms that the composer heard in his or her head and wrote down in the score.

No composer would consider it appropriate for the orchestra to play the score without a conductor, for experience shows clearly that the guiding hand that holds the baton is as essential as the great soloists and the strongest ensembles.

The same is true, of course, for the senior-most brand managers and the teams that are responsible for designing and conducting the countless actions that constitute brand management.

We think of these leaders as brand guardians, a small group, cross-functional in responsibility, who have strategic responsibilities for the delivery of brand value. The importance of brand guardians is to preside over all aspects of brand planning, brand initiatives development and execution, and to monitor and protect the expression of the brand over time. Essentially it's the same role that parents have in looking out for their children's well-being, health, development and passionate interests. The brand guardian group is like a Board of Directors with the sole task of looking intensely into the development, growth and success of the brand.

If your company doesn't have a brand guardian team, there are many good reasons why you ought to, not the least of which is the sheer importance of your brand to the success of your business. The benefits and value to the company of a strong brand are so great, and of course brand value is so significant a portion of the overall valuation of the company, that putting the best team on brand management at the highest levels is entirely logical.

Another reason to create a brand guardians group is to assure that one team is responsible for the unfolding of your brand story and how it engages with the public. This encompasses more than advertising campaign planning. The brand guardians scan for all project ideas, create new brand initiatives, and scan all marketing activities for character and story quality impressions. We'll present later in the book a set of research tools that helps this group evaluate your brand's changing position in the marketplace over time.

Promoting group alchemy is another important purpose behind the formation of the oversight group. It's helpful for the leader who brings this group together for the first time to set guidelines for how the organization intends to handle constructive criticism.

At Pixar the problem of how to fix an entertainment project that shows promise but isn't quite clicking by using "notes." Ed Catmull mentions, "A good note says what is wrong, what is missing, what isn't clear, what makes no sense. A good note is offered at a timely moment, not too late to fix a problem. A good note doesn't make demands; it doesn't even have to include a proposed fix. But, if it does, that fix is offered only to illustrate a potential solution, not to prescribe an answer. Most of all a good note is specific. 'I'm writhing with boredom,' is not a good note."

Candor is very important, and openly discussing how people feel as well as what they think is essential. Although telling the truth can be difficult, inside a creative company it's the only way to ensure excellence. This is perhaps one of the most important things that Pixar figured out, and for more than twenty years each movie the studio released was a blockbuster success. This has never been achieved in the extremely challenging and difficult world of film production, and the successful group dynamics of the Pixar Brain Trust tap into principles showing how to unlock the hidden energy of the interactive field between people working towards a common storytelling end.

The goal of the brand guardian group is to evoke and nurture profound resonance between your brand and the public. To achieve such a high state of performance, we must be able to see beyond the obvious and evoke hidden dimensions of experience, to tap into group alchemy, and to research and explore brand purpose, values, and meaning while overcoming blind spots and limiting beliefs. It is the world of brand and business blind spots that we explore next.

4 | *Blind Spots, Continuity Fields, and Assumptions*

"Noise is something that is out of place. It is usually something unwanted, inappropriate, interfering, distracting and irritating."
– David Hendy

In the previous two chapters we've discussed brands and brand resonance, and perhaps we've done so in a way that is new or surprising. It's not common to talk about branding this way, certainly not in terms of the soul and the profound impact of soul qualities, nor in terms of acoustic resonance or in comparison with Paleolithic paintings.

So it might be perfectly reasonable for you, the reader, to want to know what we, the authors, have actually accomplished in the field of branding, and how the notion of soulful branding came about. So let us now tell you how it started for us.*

The insights began to unfold at a specific company, the name of which we will reveal shortly. The company had just experienced the intense pain of its first sales contraction in its fourteen-year history. Sales had declined 10% from the previous year, necessitating a workforce reduction of 20%. Morale and confidence were at an all time low.

This came about because the company was losing market share to a key competitor, and of course the stock market had not failed to notice. All signs pointed downward.

---

* This case was originally featured in *Agile Innovation* (Wiley, 2014) by: Langdon Morris, Moses Ma and Po Chi Wu

Highlighting the problem, the company had failed to recognize a critical opportunity, and was being out-maneuvered by an emerging rival that offered products and marketing messages that were more attuned to a critical and newly emerging market segment.

The company's culture itself further complicated the uncomfortable situation. Historically distrustful of formal research and strategy consultants, management felt that they already knew what worked in the critical crucible of the real world. Key decisions about products and marketing seemed intuitive to them, which had led to bold and gutsy decisions in the past.

But in the newly competitive environment, "bold and gutsy" had slowly and inadvertently devolved into a "closed information system" that had serious blind spots and knowledge gaps. The situation was precisely as labeled by Andy Grove, the former Intel CEO, in his book Only The Paranoid Survive, a "strategic inflection point."

The obvious concern on everyone's mind was to understand what was happening in the market, and to change the direction. Whatever management chose to do, it was clear to everyone that it would most certainly be profoundly influential on the future of the organization; the pressure was on.

Conventional wisdom in marketing circles suggested that it would take this national brand two long years to reposition itself in the marketplace, which promised an excruciating and difficult process for everyone involved. Throughout the organization, the sense of dread was palpable.

The outcome that we achieved, however, exceeded even the rosiest of best-case expectations. Market erosion and the sales decline ended within six months, quickly jolting the momentum in a positive direction. The brand transformed itself by growing more than 75% per year for the following five consecutive years as revenues more than tripled, and the stock market took notice, raising the company's stock value from $5.00 per share to $35.00, largely on the strength of innovation insights and the resulting changes in marketing programs.

So let's delve into the approach and techniques that the team used to make this transformation occur, and which became the foundational insights that led to *Soulful Branding*.

Transforming Nike

The company described above is Nike, and from its very birth, the company's leaders maintained an intense focus on product design. Bill Bowerman, Nike's co-founder and the famous track coach at the University of Oregon and US Olympic team, came up with the first product ideas for the company inside the cobbler shop he ran in his garage during the late 1960s, ruining his wife's waffle iron in the process.

Product innovation became a core competence within a few years, and then the company strived to create meaningful innovations annually to serve the world's athletes.

In the early stages of growth, considerable management attention focused on finding alternative sources of production and financing, and once those problems had been solved, sales programs and systems became the big area of concern. Eventually, inventory management challenges hurt cash flow, and when some designs didn't sell very well they had to be written off.

By 1982, ten years after the company went public, Nike employed about 2,000 people and had annual sales of $693 million. It had about 1,000 stock keeping units (SKUs) in footwear, and several thousand in apparel. Creating new products was critical to the success of the company, but this is typically a messy, error-filled process.

Consequently, many packaged goods brands follow a carefully orchestrated set of product and communications research projects to reduce the risk associated with defining the new products they will roll out to the marketplace. Nike, in contrast, designed and launched thousands of new products a year; founder Phil Knight rejected the orchestrated approach to planning and felt that a traditional approach to research and product planning would paralyze the company.

Knight also recognized that if he punished designers for coming up with new products that were not a hit in the marketplace, fear would henceforth prevent them from using the full power of their intuition and imaginations, which in turn would cripple Nike's design prowess. He therefore challenged the designers, and indeed everyone working on innovation in all the company's divisions, to push themselves to explore new territory, providing this guidance to design and marketing: "just don't make the same mistake twice." It was expected that lead product designers would challenge convention and take their designs someplace new, and it was understood that this required risk taking.

This supported and enabled Nike's fluid approach to releasing new products into the marketplace four to five times a year, but to mitigate the many risks associated with this steady flow of new designs, a simple and very clever mechanism was created that helped identify what the market wanted ahead of time to reduce inventory risk.

This was the Futures Program, a footwear industry innovation. Retailers were presented with samples of forthcoming new products, and if they placed an order at least 5 to 6 months in advance they received a 10% discount and a guaranteed delivery date. This system accounted for about 80% of Nike sales, and was an incredible forecasting and risk reduction tool.

As effective as it was, however, the Futures Program could not help the company when its brand became disconnected from the needs and values of key customers. Hence, the need to reposition the Nike brand with women was the result of a ten-year, 60% contraction in sales to women. This was in direct contradiction to Nike's business strategy at that time, as the company was trying to sell more sports shoes to women during the entire period of the sales decline. It clearly just wasn't doing a very good job of it.

This blind spot gradually but significantly diminished Nike's relationship with the key women's market segment, and it finally came to a head in 1986. Jerome had just started as Nike's Global Director of Marketing Insights, and his team was charged with figuring out what was going on in the market, and what the company should do differently.

Nike's Brand Guardians

This crisis led to the creation of the very first brand guardians group, which was made up of Nike's global head of marketing Tom Clarke, Scott Bedbury, the head of advertising, Nike's advertising agency Weiden & Kennedy, Jerome as head of Marketing & Brand Planning & Research, Liz Dolan from Public Relations, Fred Schreyer of Sports Marketing, and Mark Parker of Product. Overseeing all the work produced by this extended team was Phil Knight, CEO.

This brand guardians group used semi-annual off-sites and strategic brand review meetings to discuss the state of the brand, brand initiatives, brand strength monitoring results, and future advertising plans.

But as Nike grew there was a persistent challenge to find a suitable creative structure for advanced product designs that would draw from the tuned judgment and group alchemy of Nike's lead designers. Eventually a new group emerged called the Nike Innovation Kitchen (NIK) headed by Tinker Hatfield, which took the lead in advanced design work outside the mainstream marketing and sales processes. The NIK group became the nucleus of Nike's in-house brand development studio.

During the next ten years Jerome developed tools and processes connected with the responsibilities of the Brand Guardians group, including a core set of practices based upon brand backstory research, positioning research, strategic reviews of brand strengths, weaknesses and gaps, the periodic staging of concept generation workshops to envision new brand initiatives and the vetting and presentation of those initiatives to senior management as a brand project portfolio.

As the Nike team researched the underlying issues surrounding its positioning with women and came to their provocative conclusions, the findings led functional departments throughout the company to make adjustments in their thinking, and eventually in how we communicated the core messages of the Nike brand. This process led to a speedy recovery, exponential growth, and deep insights into the very nature of branding.

Over time, these experiences provided the insights that defined the outlines of the Soulful Branding approach, and based on the work that followed and which supported the subsequent turnaround at Nike, the principles and practices of Soulful Branding were developed and eventually proven in other companies as well.

Nike founder Phil Knight played a critical role overseeing the full breadth of this work. In 1987, shortly after Jerome had moved into the planning role, Phil asked him to research the growth histories of two companies, Disney and Time, Inc. Phil wanted to know how they had achieved organic growth and what role their founders, Walt Disney and Henry Luce, had played in that process.

We gained tremendous insight into the creative process of Walt Disney from the book by Bob Thomas, *Walt Disney: An American Original.* Disney's leadership skills were extraordinary, and he was a master storyteller and story line developer. He was also a cartoonist, film technician, director, producer and salesman. Further, he cultivated his vision constantly with hobbies, projects and a cross-pollination of ideas. Disney was also a master at seeing creative potential in the people around him, and in leading projects in such a way that they pulled from people their very best work.

Phil's intuition was correct, as this review of Disney's leadership skills and his company's growth path had important implications for Nike's development. By the late 1980s, half of Disney's revenues were derived from merchandise and character merchandising connected to its movie characters, whereas Nike in the late 1980s was solely a products and merchandising company with a very weak brand storytelling capability. So one of the insights coming back to Phil was the discovery that Nike could become much better at marketing if it became better at storytelling.

Another insight was that Disney had invented the storyboard as a means of communicating the master story and key scenes in feature length films, and he also used this tool for theme park development, new park attractions and the overall development of the Disney brand. This helped Nike designers to discover storyboarding as a perfect approach to exploring design influences and story lines surrounding sports celebrities, and for exploring footwear and apparel combinations that costume a superstar in the most effective way.

Storyboarding also helps brief internal functional groups – marketing, merchandising, sales, advertising – to get new concepts green lighted for production. Nike's lead designer Tinker Hatfield possessed many leadership skills: an illustrator, designer and storyteller, and he took the lead in the use of storyboards to bring the brand character of Nike and athlete lifestyle influences into better focus. His example allowed the company to start down the path of becoming more effective in their marketing approach by capitalizing on the use of storytelling around athletic performance to enrich the soul of their company.

Nike and the Women's Market

So the segment that Nike had neglected was the women's market, which the company had thoroughly failed to understand. Like a typical celebrity standing in slack-jawed shock after his wife demands a divorce, Nike's leaders didn't understand why the company was being dumped. "We're national champions! We know sports best! Why don't you love us?"

What Nike had not understood, however, Reebok had understood exceptionally well. By 1986, aerobics exercise classes had become a national craze, particularly for women, and aerobic shoes were the primary style of sports footwear for female sports enthusiasts. The market exploded over a five year period beginning in 1982, driving Reebok from an under-the-radar brand to number one in sports shoe market share in North America by 1987.

Rob Strasser, Nike's VP of Marketing at the time commented, "We never thought that a bunch of sweaty women jumping around in a dance room would ever amount to anything." Here was a classic example of a limiting belief, and in hindsight it's easy to recognize it as an indicator of a major blind spot. At the time, however, the situation was not so obvious.

But the issue was a critical one for Nike, and the sense in the company and in the market at the time was that the future success of Nike depended precisely on figuring out what was going on, and what to do about it.

Nike experienced a 60% decline in footwear sales to women between 1976 and 1986, and it was obvious that Nike's brand positioning simply did not appeal to women. In fact, we found that it did the very opposite. By highlighting elite male athletes delivering powerful performances in various hyper-competitive sports arenas (think Air Jordan), the company's brand image was intentionally loud, aggressive, and entirely macho. Male locker-room humor and trash talking was a staple of Nike's ads, which generally worked great for Nike's key market of young males, but it alienated many women and kept Nike from realizing its sales potential to a much broader audience.

Recognizing the significance of the situation, top management called for a thorough assessment, and asked Nike's marketing and advertising groups to discover the deeper root causes.

We began by using an approach called "depth workshops*," a comprehensive process for mapping mental territories. In these workshops the marketing teams explored the mindsets of all types of consumers in and around Nike's brands, products and advertising.

The team also needed to gain a thorough understanding of the mindset of Nike's own leadership, and so we began meeting frequently with Nike executives in what turned out to be lively and animated conversations.

By going beyond the "public face" to explore the private thoughts and feelings of our own leaders, we discovered many truths that were hidden behind the choices our own executives were making. We found, for example, that the hardcore, male, testosterone-driven competitive sports ethos within the company was so pervasive that it wasn't even discussed. Like the fish in a fishbowl, we didn't recognize the water we lived in.

Another self-limiting belief concerned the design of the shoes themselves. Nike designers understood – that is, they assumed – that sports shoes needed to provide durability and high performance capabilities, with lots of cushioning and lateral stability support. The upper materials needed to be long lasting and tough.

Many women, however, felt that Nike shoes looked "clunky," that they made their feet look big, and they weren't comfortable, all negative qualities resulting from design choices that Nike's designers considered as positives. Given a better alternative from Reebok, it was no wonder that Nike's sales to women declined by 60%; but at this time no one at Nike was actually asking women about these issues. As a result, this obvious bit of market intelligence remained entirely hidden.

Reebok had seized market leadership with its Princess and Freestyle models, shoes that broke from Nike's over-engineered, high performance paradigm. With thin and pliable garment leather, Reeboks had low profile mid

---

* Depth Workshops is a term coined by the early British pioneer of qualitative research, Roy Langmaid.

soles and a minimal amount of cushioning that resulted in a comfortable shoe with a big bonus: it required no break-in period. The shoes were slender and trim, offering a more appealing petite appearance.

At the time, a debate about this raged within Nike. One side argued that Nike could never, and should never make shoes like Reeboks, because they weren't up to Nike's "high performance" standards. But of course the definition of "high performance" emanated from the macho male perspective, not from the viewpoint of the intended customers.

Once we understood the themes we should be exploring, it didn't take much analysis to formulate the questions we should be asking, questions about the objectives and motives of women participating in aerobics fitness. These were of course quite different from the objectives of young males who were participating in intensely competitive sports.

For these women, fitness was largely inner-directed, a form of therapy. It was often about personal empowerment, not high performance or competitive status, and it was done to bring a feeling of balance, play, and joy into their lives.

These emotional benefits obviously differed greatly from the competitive mindset of males, and so the product performance characteristics they preferred were also entirely different. Many women placed high value on comfort and styling that worked well for everyday wear and social situations.

Ignorance of the divergence between how men and women viewed sports, products, brands and the role they played in their lives was killing Nike's sales, just as the women's sports and fitness segment was quickly growing into the largest segment in the market.

The depth workshops uncovered these self-limiting beliefs and blind spots, and so, for the first time in its history, Nike had gained deep insight into female consumers not as statistics on a sales or media planning spreadsheet, but as athletes with attitudes and feelings about how sport, fitness, brands, products, and advertising actually and authentically fit into their lives.

It was on the basis of these insights that Nike was able to achieve a massive breakthrough; once Nike's leaders had a clear picture of just how far the company was out of alignment with market reality in so many different dimensions, including brand image, the advertising communications model, product design, and perceived product value, it became obvious why and how to change course. Nike then rapidly set about to do so.

Rather than engage in a high profile TV brand campaign, we found an unusual way to re-interpret Nike's core values into a women's narrative. W+K was briefed on the findings from the women's study and was asked to create a women's magazine print campaign to accompany Nike's best products ever for the young women's market. "The women's 'Just Do It' campaign was a mix of empathy, inspiration and empowerment" (these findings came directly out of our depth research). It spoke to women in a voice that was intimate yet strong, philosophical yet honest. W+K produced an eight-page print advertisement, "You were born a daughter," that chronicled the life of a woman using a series of statements that covered everything from first bras to first boyfriends to biological clocks to gaining acceptance of body, mind and spirit across the ages. The images presented were of everyday women (not superstar athletes) of all ages interspersed through the text. Nike's voice of authentic athletic performance had acquired a new language that was both visual and verbal.

"Of all the work we did," said Scott Bedbury, Nike's Global Advertising Director, "I am most proud of that campaign for its strategic as well as its creative brilliance."

Coincident with the running of this campaign, within a few quarters of the depth research findings coming back, the sales erosion stopped and internal metrics and external media buzz all started improving rapidly. Without any prompting from Nike, Oprah Winfrey exclaimed to her audience, "Have you seen Nike's new women's advertising campaign? OMG!" Sales to women quickly grew by more than 75% a year for the next five years in a row, and the company's stock value increased from $5.00 per share to $35.00, largely (but not solely) on the strength of sales increases to women.

The story of a brand that loses contact with its target market is not a unique one, of course, but Nike's turnaround is not so common, and that's partly why it's so relevant. Learning to re-perceive one's brand and the market eco-system surrounding it is not so easy to do, especially for established companies. But using the perceptions and methods that became the core processes used in *Soulful Branding*, Jerome and his colleagues have supported many companies, large and small, through similar transformations. Starbucks, FullSail University, and Sega are among these firms, and we will turn our attention now to Sega.

More Blind Spots: The Turnaround of Sega

In 1992 Sega trailed far behind Nintendo's share of the video game market. Both companies sold technically equivalent game consoles to similar customers, primarily young males, and they also had very similar game libraries. But Nintendo's revenues and marketing budget were several times that of Sega's, and Nintendo's lead was increasing. To survive, Sega needed a different approach, and they found it by listening more intently and purposefully to their target customers, pre-teen boys.

At the time, video game advertising was aimed at the parents, and it portrayed video games as good, clean, and largely suburban fun. This may have matched their parents' ideal, but hardly fit at all with the mentality of adolescent boys, whose instincts are more toward rebellion than suburban orderliness.

This insight led to a new Sega campaign that depicted typical teenagers having a rebelliously good time, and it resonated so deeply with their instincts that it quickly turned around Sega's fortunes. Within 18 months the company's market share surpassed Nintendo's, almost all of it attributable to its discovery of the deeper meaning of its product value proposition for its key customers through the new "rebellious" advertising campaign.

The Sega story represents another important data point surrounding the concept of resonance in relationship building. Think for a moment of the magnetic attraction that lifestyle and extreme surfers have to waves, particularly bigger waves. The pioneering big wave surfer Laird Hamilton was being interviewed once about how he came to the idea of inventing tow-in big wave surfing. He said, "I understood that the ocean was capable of producing waves much larger in size than anyone had ever surfed." This led to his invention of special surfing equipment and tow-in techniques to get positioned to ride these giants. The whole history of this sport can be seen in the documentary 'Riding Giants'. Laird's magnetic character in the waves has produced a wave of energy around the sport that has increased the Chi of the sport.

The point here for branding is that the stories we tell also produce wave forms that have a magnetic impact upon the listener or viewer. Not all stories are created equal; the skilled, creative brand storyteller is capable of producing waveforms much larger than ordinary advertisements routinely achieve.

To better understand how blind spots occur, there's a simple experiment that perhaps you remember doing in grade school: take a look at the image below with your right eye closed, and move the book toward your face with the + aimed right at the bridge of your nose.

At some point, when the book is about a foot from your eye, the happy face will disappear because you've moved its reflected light rays precisely onto your eye's blind spot. That's the specific location on the retina where the optic nerve connects, and where there are consequently no nerve cells in position to perceive the light reflected through the eye's lens from external images.

While the blind spot is there all the time, what's really interesting is that in day-to-day life your brain fills in the perception gap with the colors surrounding it, and you don't notice the blind spot at all.

In other words, your brain supplies perceptual data that the eye does not provide. In fact, the brain does more than just match background colors — every day it fills in complicated colors and patterns, flawlessly incorporating its predictions of what it should be seeing into the world before us, so skillfully that we are entirely unaware of it.

Hence, the existence of the blind spot is both an important metaphor that explains a key role that the brain plays in perception, and it's also a literal reality that we must be aware of and address.

The brain does more than this, though. It also fills in the gaps not only in vision, but also in perception. Neuroscientists tell us that the brain provides continuity to our experience by filtering out visual information that could otherwise overwhelm us, a quality they have labeled the "continuity field."* The result is that we know our mom even when her face is distorted by shadows or we're seeing her in profile." The same mechanism, though, allows Hollywood to fool us into thinking that a stunt double is the star actor. If we look closely we might see that it's not the same person, but usually we don't notice.

All too frequently, business leaders also fail to notice when the external environment changes, as Nike failed to do, which leaves them vulnerable to changes in the market.

The perception gap phenomenon has been the topic of recent research at MIT's Kanwisher Lab, where Dr. Daniel Dilks has been studying stroke patients and exploring how long it takes the brain to learn to fill in missing imagery after a stroke destroys some of its vision centers.

Using the illusion of "phantom limbs" as a reference point, which generally require about 24 hours after an amputation to manifest in the experience of the amputee, Dilks expected that it would also take hours or days for the brain to adapt to the loss of its own vision processing capabilities following a stroke.

---

* Journal of Neuroscience,. Sep 5, 2007 NIH Author Manuscript; 27(36): 9585–9594. doi:10.1523/JNEUROSCI.2650-07.2007

"I was flabbergasted," he noted, after finding that study volunteers reported seeing adjusted imagery as fast as the researchers could record it: it took two seconds, or less, for the brain to compensate.

This phenomenon, technically known as "referred sensation," gives us another piece of scientific evidence showing just how adept the brain is at fabricating its own reality. This is obviously great when you need to restore your vision, but problematic for brand directors, because to be successful the blind spots and the illusion of continuity are exactly what we have to overcome if we are to guide brand development in a changing marketplace.

We also call self-created realities "assumptions," and in business they can be deadly.

Interestingly, though, blind spots, continuity fields, and referred sensations are also very useful concepts for brand directors to utilize because they describe exactly how our customers behave; they also fill in missing data with beliefs and assumptions. Entire markets, in fact, are fully characterized by assumptions, half-truths, and unsubstantiated beliefs, so much so that perception transmutes to become reality. It requires constant attention to the market's voice to keep incorrect and distorted messages from spinning out of control, which explains why many leading brands now maintain vigilant media listening centers where alert staff members monitor news and social media 24 hours a day, and they also use sophisticated software tools such as Digimind to constantly monitor the internet.

The ubiquity and power of the Internet, and the ease of the search function, has vastly accelerated the evolution of knowledge and knowledge sharing, and consequently entire industries are now reeling from changes in consumer perceptions and tastes as our collective, connected consciousness evolves. Therefore, it has become essential for brand and marketing leaders to keep their finger on the pulse of what the public now believes about their brands, products, communications and overall value propositions, for there has never been a time in history when the mix of rational and irrational perceptions, beliefs and motives were in such a rapid state of flux.

Assumptions, then, are a sword that cuts both ways. We often discover our incorrect assumptions when they cause us to make the wrong choices, as we see with Nike and Sega. But the investigations that identify the source may then point us in the direction that leads to the solution, that is, to replace the assumptions with more substantial knowledge about what is really real.

What's essential for success is to perceive the customer's changing reality deeply and accurately, to go beyond marketplace noise and our own assumptions to see profoundly into the factors that shape consumer beliefs, as well as their feelings, behaviors, and choices. Doing so requires us to detect and overcome our own blind spots and assumptions, and as with Nike and Sega, we may also discover and create significant market opportunities and advantages as a result.

A method that we have found particularly useful for engaging in this type of work is what we call "depth research," which is our topic in the next chapter.

5 | Depth Research and the Private Voice

"The voice is not only indicative of man's character,
But an expression of his spirit,
Other sounds can be louder than the voice,
But no sound can be more living."
– Inayat Khan

The brand identities of many start-up companies emerge as an extension of their founders' visions and personalities, which are then intimately reflected in the firm's products or services, and also in its way of taking them to market. The resulting brand messaging reflects the unique ways that entrepreneurs connect their passions and drive with the qualities and values that customers really care about.

However, as companies grow, the connection to founding values and passions is often lost or forgotten, and it requires rediscovery and reinterpretation if the brand is to stay relevant with fast-changing tastes and market needs.

Understanding the intangibles that govern the strength of a brand's relationship with consumers enables brand directors to continually refocus and optimize a brand and improve its positioning. For those who are willing to delve into the deep work of hidden assumptions, tacit beliefs, private voices and unspoken feelings, we have seen this work result in spectacular and transformational business results.

How can we learn to see deeply in this way? Part of the answer is depth research, the process of exploring the hidden facets of a brand and its markets. These hidden facets frequently are understood to be blind spots, which as we discovered in the previous chapter, are often assumptions that have gone bad and have become critical inhibitors of success.

Depth research is a process that generates useful insights about the feelings and attitudes of consumers, and as we saw with Nike, these insights were about why people, all people, men and women, young and old, chose to participate in sports. Each key segment had their own needs, desires, goals, and expectations, but in assuming that their motivations were identical, Nike misled itself.

This is an important choice of words, for our assumptions generally do not arise because people try to trick us, but when we fool ourselves. In fact, when you treat people respectfully and engage them in an open and honest way in depth research, most people will readily open up with their feelings and speak to you in their "private voice," the one that reveals their true inner feelings.

In contrast, conventional top-of-mind survey work primarily reveals only the logical / rational mind or the "public voice," a much more superficial perspective that often contains many misleading distortions. Hence, when market researchers assume that people are rational and logical in their opinions and decisions, they can be fooled into thinking that the two voices (public and private) are aligned.

Human attitudes and feelings are complex and often contradictory, and the public and private voices of most people often do not speak or feel as one. This is because for most people, the public voice carries with it the need to align with others, and thus when speaking in their public voice people will frequently tell you what they expect or believe you want to hear, thereby revealing nothing of their true feelings, and in fact disguising them.

The difference between the two voices is also evident in advertising. The polite and accommodating commercial voice is commonly the language of ads, chosen with the intent to persuade strangers to take some action, typically buying a product. In Hollywood this is called being "direct and on-the-nose." There is no beating around the bush: Here's our product; here's what you can use it for; here are the functional benefits; and for a limited time only you can get it at this price.

Well over half the time, advertising fails to deliver the intended results because people have developed elaborate defense mechanisms to screen out unwanted demands upon their attention, and in the advertising context the commercial voice is precisely an unwelcome demand. Most advertising is based upon the interruption principle, and it often screams to be noticed in a radio-announcer tone (as if that tone was golden). Deeply experienced advertising producers, however, know they have about three seconds on the front end to "hook" the viewer into watching or listening to the rest of it. When the hook annoys or alienates, as it does so often, then the result is an entirely counter-productive ad whose message is "tuned out or turned off."

Depth Research through the Brand Scan

It's very helpful to learn in great depth and detail how people feel about all the brands in a given market category and how people respond to their positioning platforms, creative executions, messaging, narration and meaning. By gaining access to people's private voices, you will discover that they reveal a great deal about what is working and what isn't working across an entire spectrum of ads or brand positioning approaches that currently define the competitive category. This is the purpose of branding scanning techniques and tools that support thorough assessments of the entire marketing impressions landscape surrounding a brand and its key competitors.

When we explore and discuss what people notice, what speaks to them personally, and how they feel about it emotionally, we gain deeper insights about how to approach them in a more honest, interesting and moving dialog. This contrasts with the old model of mass marketing using mass media in a monologue radio or TV announcer style, wherein companies simply told people what they wanted to believe.

A well-executed brand scan enables planners and managers to identify the energetic qualities or elements that most powerfully influence their brands, and to discover how to add or shape greater meaning behind the brand story. This enables a brand to speak in its own private voice, gaining greater intimacy and immediacy for customers, and far transcending the superficiality of brands that communicate only in a public or commercial voice.

Through depth research, we engage consumers directly in dialog, and simply by changing the rules of the discussion we take them out of the ad critic role, and ask them instead to see themselves as the author or creator and examine how they would improve an ad or a product. This subtle change in the line of questioning yields an entirely different conversation, an authentic discussion about the full spectrum of touch points in play and the roles they play or could play in consumers' lives.

This line of inquiry reveals which elements carry the most energy and interest, providing a technique for deeper learning about the things that really move people.

Many creative people, and likewise those responsible for developing and selecting marketing ideas, dislike seeing their ideas evaluated by consumers, because it feels like listening to strangers remark about how ugly their baby is. They also dislike sharing control over the creative process with anyone outside of the core creative team. But this is generally the wrong way to look at it. Although this may sound strange to many marketers, the subject under study in depth work is not actually the advertising, nor the product, nor a rough concept. What we really care about is using those elements as stimulus to discover subtle energy shifts that occur inside of the people we're trying to reach.

Hence, this is a paradigm shift in how research can be conducted. It's the people and their authentic experiences that are primarily under study. The objects-as-stimulus – ads, products, and concepts – simply allow a conversation to take place that exposes the energy that's present on the human interactive field. Those skilled in reading body language and other signs (yawns, groans, sighs, delightful exclamations upon discovering something that resonates, etc.) will notice the volume and tone of voice and other non-verbal cues that appear in the dialog as the hidden world of magnetic energies that really engage people.

This requires, of course, that the participants trust you, understand why they are there, understand what the real goal of the research is, and open up with their feelings. If you don't know how to recruit the right kinds of people to engage in this kind of a discussion and if you don't seed the group dynamic at the front end with the right kind of preamble that sets the context for discussion in the right way, then it makes it almost impossible to shift the dialog into one that gains access to people's "private voice."

To facilitate the process it's a good idea to assemble a range of objects to use as stimuli, including artifacts from competitors, and companies in industries that you admire but don't compete with directly. The goal is to find out which ones get the emotional energy moving, which will in turn enable you to learn far more than what you might in a generic, flat discussion about likes and dislikes.

Regardless of the product or service category, after performing depth research in dozens of different industries we have found that there is really no such thing as an uninteresting product category or depth research topic.

Following a decade at Nike, Jerome next joined Starbucks as brand vice president, and he was concerned that problem solving tools like the depth workshop would not work at Starbucks. This concern centered on his understanding of sports and fitness as a very high interest and high involvement product category; it was easy to recruit people to have animated and lively conversations over a two-hour period about sports and fitness, but would that also be true for coffee?

At the time, coffee was largely sold in grocery stores, packaged in tin cans, and it became bitter and hard to drink if it sat on the burner too long. So how could you have a two-hour conversation about that?

This concern, however, proved to be completely unfounded. Until that time, coffee was mostly considered a commodity and was usually sold on price. Starbucks leaders listened more deeply and imagined more broadly to reinvent the entire category, bringing more joy, taste, romance and theatre to this market. In fact, Starbucks created an entirely new imaginary world around coffee that tapped deeply into its inherent soul qualities.

And through our depth research, we learned that the key tools used to create soulful branding at Nike also worked equally well in the coffee category.

A comprehensive Brand Scan consists of many steps, and looks at the brand, the company, and the market through many different perspectives, including steps like the Visual Brand Audit, the Product Line Review, a Competitive Brand Audit, an Online Review, and Language and Imagery Research Techniques, which are described below.

Visual Brand Audit

The visual brand audit is the study of everything that visually defines a brand. It can be as simple as a visual audit of all the brands in a category, including logos, taglines, packaging and advertising. By looking at the entire marketing mix as if it were a canvas with an oil painting on it, the patterns become more evident. So we suggest setting up a display with the history of a brand's identity and all of the competition, making it much easier to identify critical factors such as currency, staleness, color, energy, distinctiveness, voices, messages and major positioning themes. If some brands in a category are clearly leading others when you deconstruct all the brands with a visual audit, you can speculate on what elements are pulling the hardest and why. These speculations then can form hypotheses that can be explored for understanding in-depth workshops.

Leonardo da Vinci once said, concerning the art of painting and composition, that one should "go some distance away because the work appears smaller and more of it can be taken in at a glance, and a lack of harmony or proportion is rapidly seen."* In the Brand Scan, it's also easier to recognize the vital factors of meaning and character, and to see which brands are imitating the energy and positioning of leaders compared with brands that are striking out in their own original directions. In our experience, consumers usually always know which brands are authentic, original thought leaders. They also know which brands are the followers and imitators. The most creative, original, character driven brands usually have the highest margins. Derivative

---

* The Notebooks of Leonardo DaVinci http://www.ganino.com/the_notebooks_of_leonardo_da_vinci_complete_5

brands are driven more by financial considerations than upon building intangible value for the brand. Most people don't really understand intangibles so there is not much thought given to planning for their enhancement. If you are operating in a crowded category with little intangible differentiation there is enormous opportunity for new value creation using soulful branding principles, processes and techniques.

Product Line Review

Here we map the product footprint of a brand (also known as its "brand width") by comparing our product line with other brands in the same category on a number of dimensions, including segmentation around quality, price, style, and any other identifiable performance or positioning factors. This kind of review is easily accomplished on an excel spreadsheet.

This review often highlights differences between how product marketers target and segment consumers, compared with how retail sells and presents the product to them. At Nike, this scan revealed a difference that was so wide that the company's leaders felt compelled to open the company's own retail store, today known as Niketown, primarily so that the presentation of the brand and product offerings would be communicated to consumers in the most ideal light. The creation of Niketown then accelerated the evolution of merchandising throughout the sportswear industry, just as the creation of the Apple retail stores have massively impacted the retail world of personal computers, phones, music players and digital wearables.

Competitive Brand Language Audit

Here we study all the retail concepts in the category, including their logos, graphics, physical architecture, interior design styles, furniture, lighting, color schemes and unique design or experiential details such as music or digital displays to reveal the competitive dynamics and hidden competitive assumptions about what kinds of energy, values and design principles interest and engage people the most. Every 3-D environment creates an ambiance and a mood that communicates non-verbally some quality of the spirit of the brand to a person.

Adept and intelligent design has vast potential to open up huge brand gaps. It is one of the premier leverage points in branding. There are so many different kinds of design solutions possible. Some only play with surface impressions. Some designs are integrated, where form and function also perform as a moving piece of art. Some designs elevate the human spirit and speak to some intangible magnetic value that we seek but can't quite articulate. These designs embody coolness, warmth, radiance, greater performance or style. And some designs are far more knowing in regards to addressing latent and tacit needs, well ahead of anyone else.

On-line Review

Following many of the same principles of brand building in the off-line world, a brand's presence online can also be evaluated in light of developing a unique brand persona, character, values, stories and purpose.*

Regardless of the medium you are using, soulful branding is all about meaningfully connecting brands with people. Like in the bricks and mortar world, the online world is also a battle to connect with your customers in more thoughtful and inspiring ways. Digital marketing represents a new opportunity to learn new rules to be both more efficient and more effective. You still need to know whom you are targeting and how people in your category evaluate brands, products and make decisions. Each category has its own cultural quirks and conventions for what works in promoting awareness, interest, trial and repeat-purchase behaviors. Amazon has done more than perhaps any other online merchant to study the nature of the online shopper and develop new offerings, ratings and to serve up suggestive ideas.

But Amazon has also done more than almost any other online brand to commoditize the brands and products it sells. Commoditization is one of the chief enemies of any brand. It posits that the most meaningful differentiator of consumer choice is price. If your company competes primarily on low costs and low prices then you too are in the commodity business. The alternative strategy for competing is to differentiate your product on some other meaningful way than price and to tell that story in a way that matters to people.

The good news is that the online world is a brand storyteller's paradise. It presents a full palette of communications tools that will allow the adept advertising message maker or branded content storyteller to express themselves more fully than at any other time. And in this new age of online transparency, how you inform, inspire, entertain and develop your character not only still counts, it can be the major leverage point for setting your offering apart.

Word and Visual Research Techniques

Masterful researchers are familiar with a wide range of powerful research techniques: brand word association, brand human personality association,

---

* A work we recommend to go deeper into this topic is 'Webs of Influence – The Psychology of Online Influence by Nathalie Nahai, Pearson Books, 2012

brand photo sort (a large pile of random images, sorted and clustered by research participants to reveal how brands are personified or make them feel), word/adjective sorts that expose underlying relationships and associations; and dream state visualizations wherein respondents close their eyes and imagine the consumption or brand usage experience at the moment when it's as good as it gets.

Other methods include the use of drawings made by respondents that sketch key aspects of how the brand experience makes them feel. Respondents may also use images from magazines to create lifestyle collages describing how a brand fits into their lives.

This exploratory work mirrors the backstory research that a novelist might perform on his central characters to ensure that the reader continues to know the character ever-more and hopefully develop a rooting interest in that character as the plot line unfolds.

Exploration vs. Validation

Depth research is a form of exploratory research that's quite different from research done for validation purposes using focus groups. Depth workshops reveal the equities and energies invoked through different kinds of interactions, exploring consumer sensibilities that are extremely valuable in discovering where creative biases are on or off target.

Brand image, personification and characterization are examples of exploratory projection techniques in depth research. In an indirect way, talking about the public image of a set of brands in a category as if they were actual people allows you to find out the nuances in how these brands are regarded. Are they young or old, fresh or tired, attractive or unattractive? Hit brands have much in common with hit characters in popular TV shows. The public develops a rooting interest in them. They are not corny or cliché, predictable or superficial. They are attractive, sexy, intelligent, original and provocative. They have a definite point of view on life and a convincing way of getting that point of view across. They often have an underlying sense of humor and a sense of irony, which helps make them more relatable. They speak in a distinctive voice. And brand character stories, like character driven stories, are written to develop a sense of stakes. Something is at stake. In this way, they get people talking about them.

The Brand Bible or Brand Standards Manual

In addition to a greater depth of understanding concerning how customers understand and experience all of the brands in a given category, the results of this work can be used to create a Brand Standards Manual that defines clear guidelines and treatments for expressing the brand publically. Inside and outside agents like advertising agencies, sales agencies, publishing, and PR agencies would then follow these standards to ensure that the brand touch points and identity assets appear uniformly in different media channels.

Most Brand Bibles include the following elements:

An overview of the brand, including history, vision and a description of the brand personality

- Logo specifications and examples of usage
- Typography palette
- Color palette
- Image use specifications, including photography style
- Letterhead and business card design
- Design layouts and grids for print and web-based projects
- Brochure guidelines
- Specifications for signage and outdoor advertising
- Writing style and voice
- Social media guidelines

While the brand bible is absolutely needed to protect and preserve the consistency of the identity of any brand, these simple identity elements alone can only create awareness and not a deeper level of meaning and engagement. Marketing teams that merely maintain an identity without developing resonant meaning on an ongoing basis are not really increasing the intangible value of the company over time, which is one of the primary areas of focus of a really skilled brand development team.

Finding Understanding

Exploring people's reactions to creative work is thus about understanding, not about measurement, so scoring consumer responses has no place in this form of depth work. Instead, we focus on emotional understanding, feelings and attitudes as the doors into the inner and private lives of people. This requires that we are very sensitive to the energies on the interactive field between researchers and respondents.

Depth research is a quest for the discovery of meaning, a goal that's quite different from how most focus groups are set up. While validation research helps decide which of a number of product or advertising options should be put into play, the intent of depth research (aka exploratory research) is to explore and gain a deep appreciation of the private voice and inner feelings of consumers by engaging them in the search for new meaning. Hence, this kind of research requires a more patient approach, as the discussion must unfold organically. And while you should certainly have initial hypotheses about what you expect to find going into depth work, if the work is performed adeptly you'll often arrive at perspectives and truths that you had not anticipated. The point of depth research is to discover things that you had not already understood or expected.

To evoke the full depth of what is intended, analysis of depth research activities requires more than a discussion guide, exercises and a transcript of what was spoken. Instead, this interpretative discipline starts with a project brief, the hypotheses you formulate, the script you develop, and the stimuli and projective exercises you assemble. Depth research requires skillful interpretation in the set-up phase.

Those who hire qualitative research agencies to conduct the work are well advised to participate fully in all phases of the research, because this work of brand strategy formulation works best like a game of table tennis; it's ideal to bat ideas back and forth, examining unexpected evidence and evolving the brief together while continuously asking, "What does this really mean? Will this approach help us shed new light on something that we only intuitively sense as significant?"

Further, it's important to note that all the information generated in depth research is not equal. To separate the best from the merely interesting requires a kind of energy acid test that indicates salience, relevance and resonance. This requires paying attention to factors including facial expressions, body language, and voice volume or tone, which may help us discern relative emotional meanings and importance, thus providing subtle but important distinctions. These human non-verbal cues are enabling signals that can lead you to become even more present in the conversation by suggesting when to dive a little deeper through further questioning while you skim over the surface of other topics where there may be little energetic engagement.

Brand discovery depth work has some things in common with the field of Jungian psychoanalysis and transpersonal psychology. It is a form of alchemy where you can learn to squeeze gold out of shadows. And this has something to do with the nature of consciousness itself. Our subconscious mind (aka non-verbal body intelligence) speaks to our conscious minds through our moods, feelings, images and dreams. Human beings learn about their shadows when their feelings well-up or their mood changes after being exposed to threatening or negative events. We also learn about our golden world of the subtle energy body when we fall in love and project our feelings of radiant energy and love upon a loved one, a pet, a hobby or people, places and things that we become passionate about.

Depth work in brand planning is for those willing to bravely delve into the shadows of hidden assumptions, limiting beliefs, private voices, unexpressed feelings and human projections. There is much to be gained from exploring all the energies in play, the good, the bad and the ugly. By gaining access to the private voices of your prospects and customers, you can learn how to change the nature of brand communications in meaningful ways, altering the space that exists between a company and its fans or even its rejecters, a space we define as the "brand field," and which we explore in the following chapter.

6 | *The Brand Field*

"If you could harness the energy in the empty space between your cupped hands, you could boil all the oceans in the world at once."
– Nobel Laureate Physicist Richard Feynman

Quantum physicists study the behaviors of energy and matter at the atomic, subatomic, and particle levels, seeking to realize one of the greatest of human intellectual aspirations, a grand, and unified field theory, also known as a Theory Of Everything. Einstein's last years were spent in the search for such a unified field theory, and while he was not successful in his quest, those who followed have continued in this search and uncovered some pretty amazing insights about the hidden nature of reality that can have big implications for your business.

Until early in the twentieth century, a great deal of what we understood about our world was based on ideas that were formulated three hundred years earlier by Sir Isaac Newton. Newtonian physics still forms much of the backbone of modern science in a set of theories that present all the elements of the universe as physical things that are separated by space. Newton described a material world in which individual bits of matter flew around following rigid laws of motion, and the universe as a machine that worked like a clock, an idea that helped create the Industrial Revolution.

But today's physicists also see a different reality. They describe the universe not as emptiness but as a "field," a rich medium that contains hidden matter and energy and connects all of the hidden points and dimensions in space.

In a bold, brilliantly crafted page-turner that's filled with huge ideas, Lynne McTaggart reveals many of the new and unexpected dimensions of hidden energy that surrounds us all the time, in her book The Field: The Quest for the Secret Force of the Universe.* Scientists since Einstein have learned that the human mind and body are not separate from their environment, but are packets of pulsating power that are constantly interacting within a vast sea of energy and consciousness that may be the central force shaping our world. McTaggert presents many of these scientific findings, which are notable for us because they are entirely consistent with our findings in the Soulful Branding journey.

George Lucas explored this same hidden energy throughout the Star Wars series, calling it 'The Force,' while contemporary physicists use terms like *quantum fields* to describe the behavior of atomic and sub-atomic particle and wave energies.

In an electromagnetic field, for example, electrical and magnetic forces intersect through the attraction and repulsion of positively and negatively charged particles that also behave as waves of energy that move around at the speed of light.

Quantum particles are knots of energy that briefly emerge and disappear back into the underlying field. According to quantum field theory, matter does not create the field; rather the field creates matter. Hence, the sub-atomic world operates like a seething energetic maelstrom of waves, from which stuff continually materializes and dematerializes in a decidedly non-Newtonian manner.

James Clerk Maxwell, the scientist who first formulated the laws of unified electromagnetism, proposed that space was an ether of electromagnetic light, while Albert Einstein believed that space constituted a complete void. Both were subsequently proven wrong in 1911, when an experiment by Max Planck showed that "empty" space was in fact filled with particle and wave energy. Later research confirmed that in a mere cubic meter of space there is actually enough energy to boil all the oceans of the world, at once!

It may be tempting to dismiss this as irrelevant to business, but in fact it tells us something quite important. Since energy and particles materialize and dematerialize out of empty space, quantum physicists have identified a critically important fact about the underlying nature of field dynamics, which also, strikingly, has deep relevance for branding.

The significance for your business and your brand is that the world operates "inside out," for it is the fields of energy that come first, not the masses of

---

* The Field: The Quest for the Secret Force of the Universe by Lynne McTaggart, Harper, 2008, pp23 – 24

physical objects; everything exists first as vibrating energy, which is embedded in every product, communications or business construct.

Just as a spider web is built from an initial set of sticky anchor lines, and then the spider fills in the structure of the web after the anchors have been set, business concepts, products or brand initiatives reflect the great amount of intention expressed in anchor lines, those that have far more emotional energy to bring business ideas to life.

Since emotional energy and feelings develop before matter, defining the right energetic qualities and dimensions that express and produce any business concept defines what is important and significant. Consequently, it's not just a metaphor when we say that the same principles underlie interactions between people and brands as those that describe the interaction of fundamental particles. Concepts such as resonance in interpersonal relations and energy patterns, as well as profoundly human patterns including archetypes, dream states, and experiences at higher levels of feeling alive are central to the creation of compelling brands and successful companies.

The concept of consciousness is also central to managing a brand field, and thus critical for the successful management and development of any brand, since changes in individual and public consciousness always precede shifts in marketplace behavior. Hence, in this section we'll explore the connection between physics and intention.

The Mystery of Consciousness

Each human body is a corporation, one consisting of 78 organs, 206 bones, 656 muscles, 60 to 100 trillion cells, and octillions of atoms.

Each cell is a microcosm of our entire body, with all the major functions of the whole body contained within it. Our cells are encoded with all of our experiences, as each thought and memory since birth has been meticulously imprinted. Any of these uncountable memories, experiences, and sensory impressions can, under the right conditions, be randomly accessed.

All of your organs and cells are working together synergistically to make you a whole person, but science still cannot explain what consciousness is, or how the sum of our body chemicals, cells and organs produce it. Nevertheless, our own experiences tell us that consciousness exists, and we know that it has decisive influence on everything that occurs throughout human culture. Even in the marketplace there is a field of energy that largely shapes interactions with the external realities, and in this domain of energy we also know the brand field is a literal phenomenon.

In 1987 we created the first brand strength monitoring system for Nike, which helped us to explore the relationship between consumer consciousness and physical and emotional realities surrounding products and brand communication experiences.

Another great example is the Global Consciousness Project, an international, multidisciplinary collaboration of scientists and engineers who collect data continuously from a global network of random number generators that are located at 60 host sites around the world. The data are transmitted to a central archive, which contains random data created in parallel sequences of synchronized 200-bit trials every second between 1998 and 2014.*

The underlying purpose of the project is to examine the subtle presence and activity of consciousness in the world, and the scientists leading the project predicted the demonstrable existence of structure in what would otherwise be expected to be random data as collected in conjunction with major global events.

They wanted to know if it is possible that the focusing of human attention would have a measurable effect in the universe when large-scale global events occur, perhaps at a mass quantum mechanical level, which would thus prove a link between consciousness and reality.

They tested this hypothesis and found that random number generators tend to become less random when attention is focused. In other words, perhaps our collective consciousness has the ability to make reality enter a state of coherence, that is, to experience greater order.

A network of detectors around the world tests the correlation of human consciousness on a global scale in conjunction with "global events" that bring great numbers of people into shared consciousness and emotions.

The project was overseen by Dr. Roger Nelson, emeritus Professor of Aerospace Sciences and Dean of the Princeton University School of Engineering and Applied Science, who has taught and published extensively in advanced space propulsion systems, plasma dynamics, fluid mechanics, quantum mechanics, and engineering anomalies. Building on years of laboratory experiments, Dr. Nelson came up with the idea of using random event generator (REG) technology to study the effects of special states of group consciousness through instruments in 60 locations, from Alaska to Fiji, on all populated continents, and in nearly every time zone. The results show significant evidence that something remarkable happens when humans are drawn into a

---

*   Details of this project can be found at this url http://noosphere.princeton.edu/results.html

community of interest and emotion, demonstrating that human consciousness does manifest in the physical world, and thus validating the idea of the brand field as not only a concept and a metaphor, but also a physical reality. Consequently, it's critical to monitor the strength of a brand as a participant in the energy field, which means that you need to design your own brand strength monitor, a topic that will be addressed later in the book.

The Science of Consciousness

A detailed summary of research on distance healing and other effects of consciousness in scientifically measured situations is presented in Lynne Mc-Taggart's book, The Intention Experiment, which reported on the first worldwide double-blind experiments to test the power of intention.* The studies developed by McTaggart and a consortium of physicists and other scientists of consciousness research involved thousands of people around the world who sent conscious intention to targets under controlled conditions through the Intention Experiment website.

Tests developed by psychologist Dr. Gary Schwartz and his team at the Center for Advances in Consciousness and Health at the University of Arizona examined whether intention could alter bio photon emissions, the miniscule light emitted from living things, as measured by highly sensitive CCD cameras which are used by astronomers to record and photograph the faint light of outer space.

The first experiment was carried out with 400 conference attendees, who were asked to send intention to increase the light emissions of a geranium leaf, that is, to make the leaf glow. A University of Arizona lab had prepared two matched leaves with similar bio photon releases, one as subject and the other as control. Images of each leaf were simultaneously sent via the Internet from Tucson to the conference in London. After the intention period, the leaves were placed in the super-cooled digital CCD camera system and photographed for two hours. "The results of the intention were so strong that they could readily be seen in the digital bio photon images," said Dr. Schwartz.

Another study published in the peer-reviewed journal, Social Indicators Research in 1999 reported the calming influence of group meditation practice in Washington, D.C. during the period from June 7 to July 30, 1993.

The study attempted to measure the Maharishi Effect, the theory that when groups of people practice the TM-Sidhi meditation program, there is

---

* The Intention Experiment: Using Your Thoughts to Change Your Life and the World, Free Press, 2007 by Lynne McTaggart

a reduction in societal stress, crime, violence, and conflict, and an increase in coherence, positivity, and peace in society as a whole. The TM-Sidhi meditation program is practiced in groups. The Maharishi proposed that if a critical mass of one per cent of a population practiced Transcendental Meditation it would radiate a powerful influence of coherence and harmony in collective consciousness, neutralizing negative tendencies and promoting positive trends throughout both the local community and even to a lesser extent, society as a whole.

The experiment, organized by physicists John Hagelin, David W. Orme-Johnson, and Maxwell Rainforth, concluded that there was indeed a correlation between the gathering of a group of 4,000 participants in the Transcendental Meditation and TM-Sidhi programs in the District of Columbia, and a reduction in violent crime. The experiment utilized a twenty-member independent Project Review Board consisting of sociologists and criminologists from leading universities, representatives from the police department and government of the District of Columbia, and civic leaders. This Review Board approved the research protocol for the project in advance, and monitored its progress.

Drawing on terminology from quantum field theories, Hagelin suggested that the results were indeed due to the "field effect" of consciousness. "It's analogous to the way that a magnet creates an invisible field that causes iron filings to organize themselves into an orderly pattern. Similarly, these meditation techniques have been shown to create high levels of coherence in EEG brain wave patterns of individual practitioners. This increased coherence and orderliness in individual consciousness appears to spill over into society and can be measured indirectly via changes in social indices, such as reductions in the rate of violent crime. We call this phenomenon a field effect of consciousness."

In fact, according to Maharishi University researchers, more than 42 studies conducted during the past 25 years have verified the field effects of consciousness, including a study published in 1988 in the Journal of Conflict Resolution, which reported on an experiment in Jerusalem in which a group of Transcendental Meditators and TM-Sidhi program experts had assembled during the war in Lebanon. As the number of TM group practitioners peaked on several occasions during the two-month experimental period, war deaths in nearby Lebanon were found to drop correspondingly.

Orme-Johnson commented that, "The TM technique allows mental activity to settle down and transcend to a completely silent state, which is the underlying field of consciousness. When the mind quiets down to this field level of consciousness, qualities inherent in this underlying field become enlivened in individual consciousness, such as perfect order, balance, harmony, and infinite correlation. As a result, the individual becomes a transmitter of orderliness and peace in society, analogous to the way that a television or radio transmitter enlivens the electromagnetic field in a specific manner and then transmits waves through the field that can be picked up at a distance.

Evidence for the link between consciousness and the physical realm is found in Bruce Lipton's groundbreaking book The Biology of Belief, which describes how DNA is controlled by signals from outside the cell, including the energetic messages emanating from our thoughts, words, music and other frequency based energy transmissions. Using simple language and everyday examples, Lipton demonstrates how the field of epigenetics is revolutionizing our understanding of the link between mind and matter, and the profound effects it has on our personal lives and the collective life of our species. Bruce Lipton's discoveries about how our cells actually process information and energy create a very strong scientific explanation as to why people are deeply affected by the quality of the words and ideas to which they are exposed.

All of these examples tell us that there is indeed a compelling connection between what goes on in our minds and the external realities we experience in the world. Fields of consciousness exist, and they exhibit enduring influence on us all.

This will inevitably play out in the marketplace, and thus it's not an exaggeration to understand the marketplace of products, ideas and brand ideologies itself as a seething maelstrom of attraction and repulsion energies, just as the universe as seen by the physicists is exactly the same.

To apply these insights, soulful brand directors must consciously evoke the patterns of field interaction at fundamental levels, and at the same time they must consider the higher levels of human experience that are possible in the messages and stories that they bring to the market.

Further, they must recognize that every brand creates an energy field that people interact with, delivering meaningful impact on the way people think and feel. Every message, every experience, and every contact that a person has with a brand has energy associated with it, and business success is largely based upon how skillfully you create and broadcast energy frequencies, and of course how those vibrations are received, experienced, and understood.

Because people have innate sensing abilities and can perceive the difference between a mercenary message and the intention and spirit behind a message that celebrates a moment, experience or human potential, brands that operate at the mercenary level of messaging inevitably fall far short of their brand field potential.

When you learn to think about a brand as a player in the broader energy field of the marketplace, it greatly expands the possibilities to creatively solve pressing business problems and challenges because you now have access to concepts like exchange of energy, intrinsic connectedness, and the promotion of virtuous solutions that carry energy imprints related to making the world a better place.

Managing Your Brand Field

Just as the space between planets and galaxies is not empty, the space between a brand and its consumers is not empty either. It's a field, a realm that's full of subtle energies, one that is rich with many nuances and deep information, messages, ideas, desires, and opportunities. Hence, one of the best ways to generate important insights about any brand is to explore that field. All you have to do is go and look.

Within that field, the messages put out on behalf of your brand, in the form of advertising, product design, packaging, marketing displays, retail formats and all of the other forms of communication that companies initiate, interact with people in ways that may create a resonance, one that strikes emotional chords in just the right ways, just as the sound waves echo and resonate in the caves containing the great Paleolithic art works that we described in Chapter 3.

The best brands in the world do this, either through dumb luck, deep intuition, or outright skill. We advocate a powerful combination of skill and intuition, so instead of relying on blind luck it's important to examine how the many facets of exceptional brands and companies produce high levels of resonance, leading very large numbers of people to recognize these brands as the best. Resonant brands develop a halo, an aura, or mystique around their ideas and products and the feelings that people have surrounding them.

The brand field is active, energetic and alive, composed entirely of two-way communications, both overt and covert. The key elements are brand messages put out by companies, and the resulting perceptions, beliefs, attitudes, values, experiences and decisions that customers make in response, as well as the media's responses, the social media mill, rumors, competing claims and counterclaims, and even government and regulatory proclamations. While some of this cacophony occurs at an obvious sensory level of perception, most of what's really interesting is hidden and needs to be intuitively, imaginatively and creatively teased out, and thoughtfully considered.

All of this is accelerating in intensity and speed now that the Internet is thoroughly embedded in our lives, an extraordinary power that can be a boon or bane, where people are talking positively and negatively about brands non-stop, 24/7. Stakeholders are constantly forming action and advocacy groups on Facebook, posting videos on YouTube, editing/tweaking Wikipedia entries, ranting and raving in online chat rooms and forums, uploading photos on Instagram, and commenting on news sites. As a result of all this, your brand and corporate reputation is continually under evaluation, consideration, and potentially under attack.

There is an ongoing social conversation about every brand that has tremendous influence on the shape and structure of the marketplace, and it is the hidden energy source most responsible for giving life to a brand, a company, products and even whole industries. This conversation can take your prosperity away almost instantly.

For this reason, your brand character, cultivated and strengthened over time deserves to be singled out for special planning consideration, and firms that don't have a Brand Planning Director, VP or Czar who is responsible for guarding, managing and nurturing brand equity are ignoring the greatest source of wealth creation and destruction that exists today.

So while you may view the brand field as a convenient business abstraction or as a mystical abstraction, what's important is that it enables you to explore success or failure factors that largely remain hidden and unspoken. People refer to brand character using terms such as brand equity, image, trust, respect, esteem, regard, and affinity, but the deeper reality is that the inner landscape of a brand's character is every bit as deep and mysterious as any interpersonal human relationship. Indeed, any couple in love has discovered that the interactive field between I and Thou is as vast in its array of colors, tones, sensory impressions and energetic imprints as the star-filled galaxy.

As we noted in the Introduction, we are not referring to the aspect of soul that religions the world over regard as their domain, the spiritual part of a human being, regarded as immortal, but rather we are concerned with the energetic part of each person that is the seat of emotions, character and their life force. This energy dwells deep within the body's own intelligence and in the subconscious mind, the part of ourselves that we know through our moods and feelings, our inspirations and dreams, and our empathy and compassion. These are the hidden facets of our soul consciousness that puts more meaning and feeling into our lives.

The subconscious mind possesses its own form of intelligence, and scientific disciplines as well as religious and mystical traditions study this hidden intelligence and seek to explain how it works. In the East, an important facet sometimes goes by the name of Qi, Chi, or Ki, which translates as the life force that animates us and gives us consciousness. Other traditions have called this force the subtle energy body, the emotional body or the light body, while in the West some simply refer to these subtle qualities of human experience as the soul or as spirit.

Depth psychology and mythology explore soulful intelligence, sometimes expressed as a deep drive to live more fully and strive for higher ideals, the force that causes us to be moved by quintessence, by profound peak experiences and pure moments that are beautiful, good and true, where real meaning and feelings operate in human life.

Frequencies and vibrations that our hearts are in touch with guide this soulful drive, for indeed our heart is the center for a certain quality of consciousness that speaks a very different language than the rational or ego centered consciousness of the brain.

The heart, like the brain, generates a powerful electromagnetic field. Rollin McCraty, Director of Research at the Institute of HeartMath, explains in *The Energetic Heart* that, "The heart generates the largest electromagnetic field in the body. The electrical field as measured in an electrocardiogram (ECG) is about 60 times greater in amplitude than the brain waves recorded in an electroencephalogram (EEG)."

Rationality and Totems

Most marketing teams operate in a "rationalist mindset," dominated by spreadsheets, income statements, reams of market data and financial feasibility reports. Similarly, most MBA programs train future business managers primarily in the rationalist worldview, but if the rationalist worldview is the primary or the only tool for processing a brand's reality, it will likely smother cultural insights and soulful activism that can otherwise enliven the brand field.

The soulful branding mindset invites us instead to think like a mystic, an author, composer or movie producer, and also as a provocateur and cultural activist. Brand developers should treat their medium just like a novel or film project, wherein the goal is to deliver provocative information that both responds to and also triggers innate and authentic human identity needs, not trivial or destructive ones.

This distinction is reflected in the contrast between knowledge and wisdom. Knowledge is that which the head alone knows, the pursuit of which is the focus of the sciences, while wisdom is grasped by both head and heart simultaneously, and thus authentic and soulful communication and learning is only present when both the head and the heart are engaged and processing experiences at the same time.

The great depth psychologist Carl Jung taught us about the nature of each individual's soul journey by pointing out that the unconscious is a co-determining factor along with consciousness, and if we live in such a way that both the conscious and unconscious are understood and taken into account, then the personality's center of gravity shifts from being only egocentric to the point between the conscious and unconscious minds where a new type of awareness dwells. Jung names this new center of deep consciousness the "Self," while others have referred to this as the "Higher Self." This is in contrast to the lower-self, which is a construct only of the ego and rational mind.

Through our years of engagement in strategic brand studies, the idea emerged that a powerful and compelling brand is essentially a modern totem, a talisman, a special object that carries deeply personal meanings and energies. This is far from rationality, but enters deeply and provocatively into our conscious and subconscious realms at this deeper center of the Self. This suggests that customers choose a brand and its products, and use them, or in Nike's case wear them, only if the essential meaning surrounding the symbolism, its compelling character qualities, matches closely with their Self identity, which is connected to their aspirations and their personal values at a deeper level.

When customers likewise sense some nobility in a company, whose purpose and products are created in a way that respects life and has innate regard for people and human potential, this is the process of curating intangible power on the brand field. If, in contrast, nobility is missing then brand soul cannot and will not come fully alive. This is the primary source of the brand gap spoken of earlier, between the current state of a brand and its potential to develop a much higher level of intangible value and power.

This totemic quality partially explains Nike's historically strong appeal to competitive, young athletic males, for whom the brand carried deep aspirational meaning relating to heroic feats on competitive battlefields. When Nike learned to rescript its hardcore competitive male positioning by interpreting 'sports performance' in new ways, a much more broadly appealing (gender balanced) presentation of authentic athletic performance emerged. Nike then beautifully captured this new brand mantra in the iconic "Just Do It" campaign, with its energetic, inspirational and humorous calls to action across genders and dozens of different sport categories. Managing the energy in the brand field thus helped Nike solve the communications problem that was generating dis-appeal with women who did not respond favorably to Nike's hardcore ethos, and in this context the point of soulful branding is to approach branding as the development of admirable character traits and communications resonant with all the key constituents whom the brand is serving. A key element in creating such a resonance is the understanding that deep within each of us there are iconic personality traits, universal characteristics and images that we have come to know and appreciate as archetypes.

Archetypes

Everything we experience in life is imprinted into our memories, and becomes a part of our subconscious mind. Some experiences are commonly held across all of humanity, as they describe common aspects of the human journey in a single idea or image, and when these common experiences are then depicted in art or literature, which has occurred thousands of times across different cultures, then these fundamental folksy ideas are called archetypes.

Archetypes are universal ideas, experiences, and images, those that all people can understand no matter where they are from, no matter in which culture they are raised. Carl Jung was an important student of archetypes and many of the ideas presented in this section emanated from Jung. The hero, warrior, ruler, lover, and trickster are archetypes in every continent's myths and legends. The universal depiction of the mother and child is another, a pervasive subject in painting and sculpture depicted in thousands of artworks, for it, too, is a recurring life pattern and image across all cultures.

Jung pointed out that archetypes like the mother and child icon repeatedly show up not only in the arts, but also in our dreams. In fact, it is the projecting quality of our subconscious body intelligence that is responsible for the repeating patterns of archetypes in art. This suggests that archetypes are innate not only in human culture, but deep within each one of us. Today, they also appear frequently in the media, in film, and in advertising, and thus they are essential elements of branding and brand development. The most successful of them imprint messages in our individual and collective unconscious.

We see this clearly in George Lucas' Star Wars saga. Lucas quite intentionally drew upon the profound analysis developed in Joseph Campbell's masterful study of mythology and folklore, The Hero of a Thousand Faces, which describes many of the vital archetypes that appear across the ages, including the classical model of the hero that is embodied in Star Wars.

And while Luke Skywalker occupies a heroic place in the Star Wars universe, the point of an archetype is that it can apply to all of us, not just the exceptional, unique, or chosen.

Becoming a Hero at FullSail University

When students step onto the campus of FullSail University for the first time they enter a magical world of high tech sound stages, music mixing rooms, movie scoring suites, animation studios, production stages, and a movie back lot where live filming is often in progress.

In this compelling setting they embark on their own heroic journeys, their own quest to transcend the dark side and bring more order and force into their own personal universes. They discover that the university faculty are their allies, mentors and guides, their Yoda, and the many high tech classrooms are the mythical planets and caves that these young heroes must master to find hidden secrets that will unlock their latent creative powers.

In 2004 the leaders of FullSail University, now the world's largest Entertainment Media Arts school, began to think more expansively about how their brand might be developed to achieve its full potential and become one of the world's finest entertainment media arts colleges. In 2004 there were over one thousand colleges in the US that were teaching courses similar to what FullSail offered. As they worked through the archetypes that typify the educational journey, and which would resonate most deeply with the young people they wanted to attract to the university, the metaphor of the heroic journey came into focus.

By working closely with FullSail's leadership team, we helped them discover the full potential of their brand, and after five years of concerted effort Full-Sail had transitioned from a trade school to a full-blown university, expanding from 5 to 40 undergraduate degree programs and adding several master's degrees. The campus architecture was completely transformed from a strip mall and business park architecture to resemble a movie company back lot, with palm trees, electric cars, bicycles, outdoor and indoor theatres, a stadium jumbo-tron and ticker-tape parades to announce, display, and celebrate exceptional student work. The student population during these 5 years swelled from 4,700 to over 22,000, and the average tuition to graduate nearly doubled.

Brand communications were transformed from simple descriptions of the programs and syllabus, to detailed materials anticipating and addressing the unspoken concerns and fears of prospective students and their parents.

One communications initiative explored the emotional power and gravity of the entertainment industry, while another compiled statistics related to job placement, starting salaries and career earnings potential to bring reality to the dreams of what might be, to help prospects and parents reflect upon this very important, emotional and high cost career decision.

FullSail conducted monthly open houses of its campus for prospective students and their parents, and these events staged and featured the many ways that the university could help their student prospects to succeed. Prospective students walked the campus, met teachers, saw examples of the current student work, and talked with the college placement department staff of 35, all dedicated to helping each graduate chart a successful career course. All of these efforts added meaningful substance to FullSail's motto, "If you're serious about your dream, we'll take your dream seriously."

FullSail applied many of the same entertainment industry skills to present its own story in person and on its award winning website. Live band performances brought sound stages to life; polished entertainment skills were expressed through presentations, building architecture and the campus design overall, in total a remarkable example of soulful branding initiatives conceived and well executed over a relatively short period of time, and their success demonstrates the importance of having a clear view of the brand field, and a commitment to managing it well.

We were engaged for four years to help guide the executive team of Full-Sail with this multi-year brand development project. The Soulful Branding principles and process presented in this book were employed in this brand development work.

One of the most gratifying things that can occur in a project of this magnitude is that this sort of work accomplishes multiple goals simultaneously. In kicking off the brand development process, Jerome assembled the top dozen executives of the school in one morning and provided an overview of what branding is all about. Then he led the group executives in concept generation work. In the span of two hours the core group of brand guardians (the top executives running the school) produced 331 ideas for how the school might be improved. We broke them up into three groups and gave the same list of 331 ideas to each group. Group A was asked to find the top ten ideas that would increase sales. Group B was asked to find the top ten ideas that increase the brand's image. Group C was asked to find the top ten ideas that would strengthen the internal culture of the company. After 90 minutes of sorting things out, we assembled the groups in common session and posted their top ten lists side by side.

The owners of the school were very surprised to find that in each of the separately derived lists, the same six projects were listed. In other words, it is possible to identify brand initiatives that simultaneously grow sales, elevate the brand's image and strengthen the internal culture of the company.

When brand planning proceeds from a strong understanding of mission, purpose and values at the very core of the brand, a higher level of synergy and resonance is possible in brand development work.

7 | *Field Exercises for Brand Planners*

> *"Hold fast to dreams, for when dreams go, life is a barren field, frozen with*
> *snow."*
> – Langston Hughes

The principles of soulful branding are based on the reality of interactive fields, and the importance of love, respect, and regard for one another. Instead of filtering reality to see only a superficial, mercenary or arms-length transaction reality, soulful brands express their brand strength through multi-dimensional intimacy. Hence, soulful branding means using insight into the nature of interactive field energy in human relationships to advance business performance.

This approach to brand planning goes far beyond writing an advertising brief and outsourcing the communications work to an external agency. Instead, it challenges the executive team to look inside of themselves and take responsibility for defining and articulating a brand character with depth and multiple dimensions, and forming ideas and brand initiatives around quintessential or archetypical experiences.

What follows in this chapter is a series of brand ideation exercises in the form of questions and metaphors that prompt you to examine your brand concept from multiple perspectives. These questions are best pondered when you have time to ponder them, not when you're rushed from one to-do list item to another. Pondering the questions is best done when the mind is in more of an alpha wave state, not Beta-locked which only uses half of your brain. These are excellent questions to use in a strategic brand planning offsite, getting a small group of strategic thinkers out of the office for a day or two to examine strategic questions more deeply to strengthen sales, the brand image and company culture. Mixing up such an offsite with unstructured individual and group time outdoors can be very helpful to reducing stress and allowing brain waves to slow down so whole-brain processing power can be easily accessed. Mindfulness exercises and meditation facilitate entering an Alpha brainwave zone.

1. Fields of Play

In your mind's eye, map your brand's "fields of play" to identify the energy and leverage points that exist within and around your business concept. How are you currently segmenting your marketplace? Can you bring your consumer profiles to life through a broader and deeper understanding of why people engage in the category? What are the key performance dimensions where competitors are fighting for recognition and market share? What brand dynamics are driving change?

2. Let Energy Guide You

The most intensely studied fields in quantum physics are gravity, electricity and magnetism, and you can use these energy concepts as metaphors for your business or brand field concept. From a customer perspective, where does the most gravity exist? From a customer perspective, where does the most gravity exist, that is, to what locations in the overall brand field are customers drawn? Where is the most electrical energy in category communications, that is, where is the market place most alive? Which firms generate the highest level of energy in the category? How can you make your brand concept more magnetic?

3. The Dual Deep Dive

Two particular brand fields require deep dive analysis to solve the problems that are often most difficult:

(a) A business leader's own "self-awareness field" contains assumptions and tacit beliefs that perhaps once served the company well, but may now be limiting beliefs. Do you know where your hidden assumptions and blind spots are? What learning initiatives can be defined and employed to erase them? These questions are excellent ones for a politically neutral moderator to help the group explore in a brainstorming session using cluster-charting techniques.

(b) The "consumer field" is as complex as consciousness itself, a profoundly deep well of knowledge, intuition, beliefs, and motives. If your business is in decline, you may be able to learn why by studying the consumer and brand fields simultaneously. As a brand is a convenient "vessel" made up of all the touch points and experiences people have had with your company and other companies in the category, adeptly exploring the nature of your brand's meaning can be the fastest and most accurate approach to finding where brand field energy may be weak or out-of-balance with the needs and expectations of the marketplace.

4. The Higgs-Boson Metaphor

The recently discovered Higgs-Boson particle is the hidden energy in the universe that gives mass to all things. Metaphorically, consider what gives mass to your business model or product concept. What leverage points (particle and wave energy – i.e. physical & emotional energy) in your marketing mix are creating the most value in the consumer's eye?

You can identify these hidden energies for your own brand or other brands that may be giving you trouble. You can intuitively zero in on what energies or factors are materializing success in the hidden web of business relationship that make up the brand fields in the category. Many companies have only direct product associations to point to in locating their brand mass, but if your company is doing only product positioning you have a great opportunity to create deeper understanding around new brand initiatives that target a higher set of human values and experience.

5. The Heart Field

Quantum fields are shaped by energy and frequency, not by physical force. Only love can win over another human heart, never force. The war on evil is a misnomer. Physical destruction only breeds more of the same. All people contain within themselves quantum fields where the human heart is the largest and most powerful organ for processing all of our experiences. Feelings are energy! So it's not just what you say, but also how you say it that matters. Non-verbal cues, tone, and intention enable us to sense the quality and depth of regard as a form of energy between people, or between companies and people. What is your company's level of regard for the people you are serving? How are you communicating the high regard that you have for the people who give life to your company and brand? This is also a helpful exercise for politicians to consider when the relationship between two nations is suffering, as the same observations and principles apply.

6. Group or Segment Attraction

Attraction and repulsion are energetic properties in the quantum field, and they are also energetic properties in your business; your goal is obviously to minimize repulsion and increase attraction. Nike didn't realize that it was actually repulsing women with its brand image, advertising messages, product design qualities and overall price/value proposition. Do you have customer groups or key constituents whose needs you do not intimately understand? Of the groups that are most attracted to you, can you clearly point to the strengths that create that magnetic affect? Can you use those strengths and build upon them to take your brand relationships to new heights? Good brand strategy usually starts with identifying your strengths so you can contemplate how to build upon them.

7. New Ideas

In the quantum field, particles are born, decay and then die, only to be reborn again; business models and brands behave the same way. Quantum mechanics show us that new particles, new energy packets, are materializing out of the hidden energy of the quantum field all the time. In the same way, a business can tap into the latent creative powers of its employees or consultants to bring new ideas into reality out of thin air. All it takes to do this is to assemble a group of people and ask them the right questions, and then let the subconscious mind and creative expertise of a group go to work to uncover new solutions and answers. There is an art to setting up concept generation sessions that increase the likelihood of arriving at new, highly valuable brand initiatives. If your company has never done this kind of work before, it is generally very worthwhile to look outside the company for guidance in setting up this kind of work. Once you've been through ideation several different times, using various kinds of mind-burst exercises, you'll quickly grasp how to set up this kind of work internally in the future when its needed.

8. Raising Your Vibrational Frequency

Consider particle and wave energies. Quantum and brand fields both contain two fundamental energy types, particles and waves. In business, particles are the physical things that the business produces, manages and controls: products, inventory, employees, buildings, and money. Wave energy is experienced in things like how you regard people. This starts with how leaders regard and treat employees, and in turn how employees regard and treat customers. Wave energy is also present in all corporate, marketing and brand communications, in creative design, architecture, the staging and mediation of corporate events and sales meetings, and in the articulation of a company's very purpose and involvement with the community. Today, most companies are really good at managing physical things, particles, and yet not as well developed in understanding the wave energy and frequencies they are creating. Consider how the vibrational frequencies, the wave energy your brand is producing can be raised or brought into a greater sense of harmony or resonance. There are many levels to this kind of work. Strategic planning in this area is best left to people with highly refined relationship, artistic and creative sensitivities. People who are not good at reading the emotional energy in others, who are more caught up in their own world of needs and drives are not well-suited for this kind of work, unless they enter the creative team with a certain level of openness and a willingness to learn.

9. Quantum Phase Coherence

When a set of brand values are consistently delivered across product design, production, sales, marketing, communications, brand storytelling, and company purpose, the synchronized energy creates a highly coherent wave form that delivers to customers integrated brand value. In quantum coherence, sub-atomic particles cooperate with each other, as it's possible for particle and wave energies to communicate and resonate together. Like a multitude of tuning forks resonating together, many waves in sync create one giant wave. When a business is functioning smoothly and in harmony in this way, the power of this congruent wave energy emanating from your brand's DNA provides a positioning power in the marketplace that is not achievable by any other means. This is a deeper meaning behind the concept of business synergy.

These are just some of the many questions you can and should ask yourself as you begin to explore the essential power and character of hidden energy as a critical force in defining your brand and communicating its value. Now we will turn our attention to the systematic process we engage when we're conducting a thorough, top-to-bottom review of a brand's design, performance and possibilities, the brand field review.

8 | *The Brand Field Review*

"Seeing reality for what it is is what we call discern-
ment. The work of discernment is very hard.."
— Lewis B. Smedes

Our research into the nature of fields and field dynamics within business confirmed the findings of the physicists and the mystics, that we live in a vast sea of energy and light, and that the hidden force that sustains the Universe is around us and inside us all the time. Coherent fields surround and permeate all living organisms, including businesses, brands and people. Living things can re-pattern life structures within themselves as an act of will; we are all connected to hidden life forces and have transformational capabilities to raise our level of Qi, or life force energy.

Through years of performing many different kinds of brand research, we also came to understand how a brand acts like a vessel or container, one that holds meaningful as well as irritating imprints that customers experience and remember and which then have significant influence on subsequent attitudes and choices.

For FullSail, that container was a promise implied to young students and to their parents about the kind of experience they would have during their college years, and the value of that experience in the job market once they were done. University life is certainly a period of transformation in the life of a young person, and so it fits the metaphor of the hero's journey, matching the brand image quite well.

But what if the brand identity of a firm is ambiguous, or is simply not fitting at all with the intended business purpose? While we're not proposing that you show up at the next meeting of the executive committee and intone in a deep and resonant voice, "I sense a disturbance in The Force," we are suggesting that by tapping into the field of the collective unconscious you can discover new ways to articulate and enhance the meaning of your brand, and improve its market performance.

In this chapter we explore seven key dimensions of strategic brand planning that constitute a large part of the brand field: brand, customer, enterprise, regard, voice, imagination and purpose. Each of these seven subjects addresses a specific "field" of hidden energy and ideas that can be strategically reviewed, and where necessary, massaged or re-arranged to create more virtuous effects and more powerful business results.

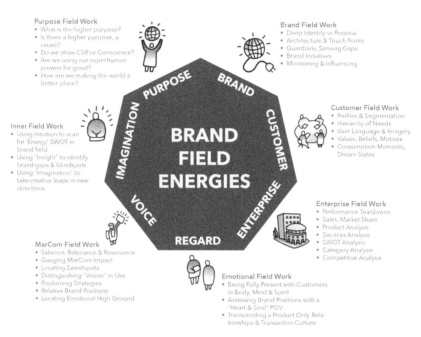

Figure 2. Brand Field Energies

The Brand Field Review is a process and a discipline that enables you to explore and understand your own brand and the hidden energy dynamics of all the brands in a category. By learning which brands have the strongest relationships with consumers, and the nature of hidden beliefs about each brand's personality and character, you can significantly improve your own brand initiatives by communicating more effectively.

1. The Brand Field

As we mentioned, a brand is essentially a totem, a contemporary talisman that may carry a deeply personal meaning for your customers.

People choose a brand, use it, watch it, wear it or patronize it to express their own inner world, but only if the essence of a brand matches some aspect of their self-identity, values, aspirations or life goals. This is true to a degree of all brands, and it is particularly important for brands competing in the culture industries, including personal technology, entertainment, clothing, beauty, fashion, auto, food, beverage, hospitality, tourism and education.

The consumer is in control of their own body, image and space, and we must be present with them to understand their needs and their mindset as we enter their world. Hence, one of the most important factors to consider when managing a brand is that when a consumer chooses a product, attaches it to their body or takes it into their home or office, the brand becomes a part of their identity and also a guest in their personal domain, and entry there is only by invitation. Thus, the relationship between a brand and its family of dedicated users is first of all a relationship of symbolism and meaning. Therefore, the study of symbolism is an essential element in the art and practice of brand management.

The following exercise, best for 5 or 6 people may help you better understand what any brand stands for by using simple word associations to explore the personality of the brand. Draw a circle in the center of a flipchart or white board and write your brand name inside the circle. Ask the group to call out the images, words, products and other key associations that come to mind. Any brand that has history and a rich set of associations will inspire a rich set of concepts in 5 to 10 minutes at most.

Use a second set of questions and a fresh sheet of paper and ask, "If this brand were a person, what kind of a person would it be? Male or female? Young or old? Attractive or repulsive? Darth Vader or Luke Skywalker?" Keep going with this personification line of questioning until you get a good feeling for what kind of character this brand really represents.

If this brand were a person, what are the words and actions that describe it best? How does it regard its fellow human beings? How does it regard nature? How does it regard its own community and workforce? It's OK to get intuitive impressions based upon feelings. Just because an advertisement or article was written about character related questions doesn't mean they can't be asked.

Does this brand consider customers as intelligent or stupid? Would you characterize the brand as attractive and someone you'd like to get to know better? Is it warm and human, or wearing a mask and hiding something? Are communications from the brand relevant to you personally, and emotionally positive? Or are any of the brand messages irritating or off-putting?

The interesting thing about this simple brand personification exercise is that the results you get will differ if it is done with company staff, or with externally recruited participants.

Results also tend to differ if this exercise is performed with young people as compared with older people, and they will likely differ again if it is performed with men versus women, or if the consumers you recruit are heavy versus light product users, or located in a different country.

Brand defectors can be especially valuable to engage, as they are familiar with the brands in a category. Exploring their reasons for switching can expose information that is incredibly valuable. Once you know what causes people to leave a brand, then you can begin working on strategies to win them back. This is only true for a brand where fundamental trust has not been violated.

What these questions and themes identify are the gaps between what management and employees think and feel a brand stands for, and what other people outside the organization think and feel. Identifying internal and external brand position differences is an important step in understanding your brand gaps and what new directions are needed to close the gap if your brand falls short of your internally envisioned ideal.

Then you're in a position to develop brand strategies and brand initiatives that can move your brand positioning forward in a positive, charming and appealing direction.

2. The Consumer Field

Understanding the relative positions of all brands in a category can be one of the most powerful strategic research tools any company can possess. Consumer tastes, preferences and behavior are also subject to change when value propositions in the marketplace change, and these changes can creep up on you in a very silent but deadly way if you're not alert.

The consumer review thus considers how competing companies and their brands constitute the consumer decision set in a given category, and how the specific brands and products are present in the lives of consumers, and why these consumers make their brand choices. We also examine the emotions that are associated with the most desired products, and seek to identify peak experiences, dreams, ideal outcomes, as well as failures and disappointments.

The right respondents will be active participants in reviewing all these subjects, with knowledge of multiple brands, and in the early phase of research it is important to find out which brands can be recalled without stimulus. If the category under review is sports and fitness brands, the first questions would not ask people to name any brands, but would rather ask, "What role do sports and fitness activities play in your life?" This allows people to reveal how they are connected to the category through factors such as thoughts, feelings, habits and behaviors. Respondents can be recruited based upon different levels of knowledge and involvement within a category.

General questions also allow them to reveal their own genuine language, not trade speak or advertising speak, and to describe their own imagery and intensity of feelings for the role that particular activities play in their lives.

A small group of people can listen to one another and dialog together, creating in effect a depth workshop to explore the inner world of human experiences, beliefs, attitudes, values and behaviors.

Sometimes there are substitute products that may not at first glance appear to be competing with your brand for sales, but a deeper examination may tell a different story. Nike assumed in its early phase of growth that people purchased sport shoes primarily for their specific design purpose. But, if you actually went out into America and interviewed people, you found many cases of people running in tennis shoes or going to aerobics in running shoes. It can be very revealing to learn that people in the real world don't think, feel or behave based upon the kinds of things that are projected in advertising within the category.

3. The Business Field

The annual process of identifying how to boost performance starts by looking at business results and comparing actual results with budgeted results. From this review it's generally easy to identify strengths, weaknesses, opportunities and threats, also known as SWOT.

An old and very valid truth in building strong brands is that you need to understand your strengths first, and you should set a priority on building upon them. A marketing SWOT analysis can help you drill down into your internal organizational strengths and weaknesses. The energies in play across the marketing mix are plotted on a chart to identify where you feel your brand is ahead, equal to or behind the competition in important dimensions. Doing this well requires intimacy with the entire category, as well as intellectual honesty and the willingness to size up your brand against the strongest competitive brands in the category.

4. The Heart Field

Assessing the public voice of your company to detect a purpose and tone that reveals a more human set of values than making money is what the heart review is all about. What kind of tone and content are you putting out there?

Is it celebratory? Are you sharing your passion behind your purpose? Is your articulation of your company and brand truth merely factual and descriptive? When heart energy is used in an open and engaging way, the energy in a brand's interactive field can expand dramatically; the easiest way to assess whether or not the brands in a category have emotional resonance is to conduct a brand position analysis as described above, as it reveals what people associate with your company and brand, helping you determine how they regard you as a brand. If they are merely aware of who you are and what you do, but have little or no feelings about their relationship with your brand, then you haven't engaged with heart energy.

The steps a company can take to perform a heart field review should include triangulating one's brand purpose first. An example of how to do this was presented earlier with Nike and how it arrived at "Just Do It." Early stage companies can also develop and articulate a compelling point of view on their purpose, values and beliefs that gives the public a clear idea of the heart energy behind the company. If the founders have an absolute passion for producing a certain kind of product or customer experience, then find inspiring ways to translate these values into statements or stories that support your beliefs.

5. The Communication Field

Here we investigate the power of a brand's voice in all marketing communication materials, and compare it with competitive brands within the category. Spectrum analysis scans for salience, relevance and resonance and identifies which ads are authentically breaking through, standing out, saying something important, striking emotional chords, and leaving strong, positive brand imprints.

Communication field analysis can be performed in any medium, including TV, video, print and websites, even where different types of branded content may be on display.

Further, it can be conducted at the brand level or the product level, by specific segments of consumers (men vs. women for instance).

A prerequisite for getting clear and accurate results is to assemble all the relevant ads from the relevant channels. Based upon your own reaction to these ads, form hypotheses about which ads have the most and least punch, which are the most credible, which strike the deepest emotions, and what positioning themes are in play.

This communications field review exercise can be very helpful if done when new ad briefs or campaigns need to be developed.

It can also be helpful in reviewing the overall efficacy of current advertising strategy and model with the public at large or with specific segments, allowing you to identify major positioning themes and creative approaches at work in the category, and from this knowledge you can look for gaps and unfulfilled category potential.

6. Inner Fields of Innovation and Creativity

There are times when a brand team needs to rejuvenate the brand. The goal here is to draw upon your own intuition and imagination to take creative leaps and move a brand forward in new ways that may surprise, delight and satisfy your consumers in new ways. This is particularly valuable in fast moving consumer goods categories that frequently refresh, revise, or update their brand positioning strategies, and it's essential for any brand whose positioning has fallen behind the category leaders and needs to be rejuvenated with fresh ideas.

The brand guardians group, mentioned above, should take responsibility for key facets of the evolution of your brand innovation and creative expression. As we noted, this team is generally drawn from a cross-section of leaders at senior levels of responsibility. In the Strategic Brand Planning process chart below, the Inner Field Review can also go by names such as Brand Concept Generation or Brand Initiatives Ideation. If your company has ever conducted a Marketing or Product Concept Generation session, the Brand Initiatives session can follow a similar format but the focus is to strengthen and grow the company, brand strength and the strength of the internal culture.

Usually this kind of a workshop takes at least a month to plan. The brand guardians are invited plus a few selected others who have deep expertise in areas that may need exploration. The session usually starts off with a state of the brand presentation and a call to action related to the need for rejuvenation and development. Then this group is led by a moderator, through a series of mind burst exercises that quickly tap into the instincts, intuition and experience of all present. The goal of all mind burst exercises is to generate seed concepts, usually collected on 3 x 5 index cards as statements or phrases. After several hours of mind burst exercises with a group of 8 – 10 people it is not unusual to generate over 300 new ideas for how to strengthen the culture and brand and grow sales.

After a sufficient number of seed concepts exist, then the group sorts and ranks the list of concepts, to find the biggest and brightest ones. Usually the screening criteria at this stage are also intuitive; gut instincts on cost and benefit, brand fit, operational complexity, image power and cultural factors come into play. The initial screen is a much broader filter than financial only considerations.

With the help of a moderator, the brand guardians group can be led to agree as a group on the reduction of over 300 ideas into a top ten or a top five list. This short list can be divided up by the brand guardians who then go into break-out groups to discuss how they would consider executing and communicating the brand initiative to senior management who must ultimately dispose of the suggested business development enhancements in one of three ways: Green light it, Red light it, Yellow light it.

A Green light means the idea is approved for full business case development. That means it needs to be defined and managed as a discrete project, with a budget, project lead, calendar, and reports to the brand guardians on the status of the initiative and eventual impact on brand strength as measured in a tool like the 'Brand Strength Monitor.'

7. Purposes and Vision Field

The final review stage is to examine the mission and vision of a company beyond its sales and profits, to explore the inner goals and purposes. Great brands are driven by great purposes, not just producing profits but also making a profound difference in society. Many great brands gain traction in their early days because their leaders have identified some hidden need that is aspirational, as Apple did in the early days of the personal computing revolution with its statement, "The Power To Be Your Best." From the very start the company empowered people with creative tools to help them express their passions and change their world for the better.

The product, the personal computer, extended the reach of an individual's power to get things done, to communicate more persuasively, to compose beautiful documents and beautiful pictures, to perform research from the desk, amongst many other liberating and empowering functions.

At its beginning, Nike was a running shoe company, and even with a single line of products the company's leaders knew their purpose was to help athletes extend their range and achieve higher performance without injury. Its internal brand mantra was developed a few years later when more product lines were developed, expanding its purpose to encompass innovation and inspiration for the athlete in each of us by enabling "authentic athletic performance" as its core organizing, design and innovation principle.

Corporate mission statements often define and describe what the company does, its scope and goals, but usually more from an investor perspective. The actions needed in a Purpose or Vision Review are revealed by assessing how the corporate and brand purpose is communicated to inspire and entertain consumers. The consumer-oriented brand purpose brief is a very different brief than an investor brief. Many companies don't make this perspective shift distinction.

As was mentioned in the *Just Do It* example, this is a process that often requires context and the triangulation of different spheres of influence to really locate the brand's core purpose and define it in an inspirational way. Simon Senek delivered a TED talk entitled, "How Great Leaders Inspire Action" that spoke directly to the challenge of describing your company purpose in just the right way.*

Regardless of the commercial business purpose, all organizations are really in the people business first, simply because they have to serve people in order to prosper. From this perspective, all marketing is therefore about nurturing and developing human relationships, and thus all facets of the Brand Field Review Exercise enable leaders to reflect on how their brands are touching the people they intend to serve. Brand leaders should always be aware of the quality of their touch and which touch points have the most leverage and are the most irritating.

Each of the seven focus areas provides a different lens on how people sense and process important information and feelings about the companies and brands that they work in, compete against, or select, so reviewing how your brand is differentiated along each of these dimensions will certainly give you new ideas for how to develop a more strategic and soulful brand. Ultimately, brand field analysis, brand guardians and brand initiatives will help you map the gap between the current state of your business and its future potential, and design a brand development roadmap or route map to greater prosperity.

Simplifying Complexity

If you are new to brand planning, development and management then the seven field exercise framework may appear to be complicated, but given how important a strong brand is to a company's position in the marketplace and to its valuation, it quickly becomes apparent that an undeveloped brand plan or strategy is not a viable option. Too much is at stake.

---

* How Great Leaders Inspire Action – Simon Senek: http://www.ted.com/talks/simon_sinek_how_great_leaders_inspire_action?language=en

9 | *The Power of Storytelling*

"You may tell a tale that takes up residence in someone's soul, becomes their blood and self and purpose. That tale will move them and drive them and who knows what they might do because of it, because of your words. That is your role, your gift."
— Erin Morgenstern

One of the enduring and universal stories in all human history is the story of love. For thousands and probably tens of thousands of years, the stories of love won, love lost, love requited and unrequited have constituted one of the most important of all themes, not only reflecting human intent and aspiration, but also shaping it. An authentic love experience is a life-transforming event, and ignites the strongest magnetic charges of human attraction on the interactive field.

The astute brand manager therefore will, sooner or later, wonder why it is that people are so often changed by the stories they hear, and also wonder how to link their own brand identities to the stories that are reflected in universal human consciousness. To understand this critical factor, it's helpful to look inside the functioning of the human brain.

Paul Zak, director of the Center for Neuroeconomic Studies at Claremont Graduate University conducted a fascinating experiment in which he sought to link consciousness with physiology. He showed participants a short animated story about a boy and a father who was struggling with cancer and then asked them to donate money to strangers. Some did so quite willingly, and to see if this could be measured physiologically, blood samples were taken from the participants before and after the experiment.

The samples revealed that the story itself had led to higher levels of both cortisol and oxytocin in many of them. Cortisol is a hormone that focuses our attention, and is also linked to experiencing distress, while oxytocin is associated with care, connection and the feeling of empathy. Those who experienced increases in both cortisol and oxytocin were more likely to donate generously, showing quite clearly that storytelling can indeed create behavioral change by literally altering our brain chemistry.

Hence, stories evoke a strong neurological response that may then be reflected in body chemistry.

Stories that deliver some kind of emotional content are also strongly connected with memory. Frequently the human mind attempts to remember information by assembling pieces of experience into a story, by combining desire, life objectives, and then searching how to overcome obstacles in the narrative format. Stories are what we remember, while most of us quite quickly forget lists, bullet points and merely factual product or business information.

Joseph Campbell once said, "There is a theory going around in education circles that the character of the teacher doesn't matter so long as the teacher has the information and imparts it. This theory is wrong! It is the character of the teacher that evokes emotion in the student. Without that element, emotional participation and identification with the learning is missing. Without an emotional component in learning, knowledge and wisdom is not fully assimilated. Everyone can remember four or five teachers out of dozens that they had who actually did something for them. These extraordinary teachers with strong characters are people who evoke one's self-image."*

Consequently, if you're responsible for marketing communications and you develop web text and provide reports filled with bulleted lists and statistics, your findings will likely go in one ear and out the other, regardless of how compelling the numbers may be. But if you can find a story that reveals the character and emotion behind the numbers, and you present that story with pathos and personal style, then your work will be much more memorable and effective.

Similarly, if you're a business leader, a big part of your job is to create an organization that takes the right actions, so just focusing on specifications and descriptions of products or functional tasks will be of limited value, while crafting an inspiring story that moves people on some level will be far more attractive and motivating.

---

* Joseph Campbell – Mythos Lectures on DVD 2012

Human stories with emotion create connections by defining the context that people need to locate themselves within a larger experience, and all great brands have found the way to create compelling stories with emotional cues that build their image, mystique and magic.

Storytelling at Disneyland

Walt Disney's initial experience and expertise was in making cartoons, and although he created Disneyland, he was not trained as a theme park designer, social architect, or civil engineer. But he was a creative visionary, a soulful leader, and dreamer who challenged his teams to stretch towards new forms of entertainment, creating in the process an entertainment brand unlike anything that had come before.

Disney's vision was his personal quest, to create fantasy worlds that make people happy by entertaining them in a funny, compelling and heartfelt way. To this end he developed characters with pathos and heart so audiences would develop a deep interest in the dramatic outcome of his stories. After many years of cartoon making he came to understand that he wanted his company and trademark to become known as "The Premiere Storytelling Entertainer, "and he never lost sight of this vision as the Disney Company expanded and evolved over many decades.*

Walt Disney, the brand visionary, created a compelling future for his company and for the entire entertainment industry by guarding and guiding what 'Walt Disney Presents' would come to mean in defining a brand of fun, family entertainment, and he used his storytelling skills to inspire people to join him in fulfilling his dreams.

The Disney organization created many innovations in storytelling and film production: new animation techniques to achieve greater realism, an artistically unique style and storytelling ingenuity through the invention of storyboards and stop motion photography as an aid to animation. The Disney studio was the first to match sound to movies.

He established artistic quality standards and a scientific approach to animation, and created a new university to teach those techniques. The Disney organization invented Technicolor so cartoons could be seen in color, and invented countless wonderful stories and characters, all toward the end of "making people happy."

About twenty-five years after he founded Walt Disney Studios, Disney realized that he needed to diversify the company; his search for inspiration took

---

* Walt Disney: An American Original' by Bob Thomas, Simon & Schuster, 1976

him all over the world. Disneyland itself was largely inspired by Tivoli Gardens in Copenhagen. Through his studies, Disney gradually came to understand his goal, "to create a living, ever-changing entertainment." Later, while on a South American goodwill tour during World War II, he found the inspiration for the Disneyland feature rides *Pirates of the Caribbean*, the *Jungle Cruise*, and the *Tiki Room*, and his personal fascination and hobby with quarter-scale model trains also led to several theme park rides.

Disney also pioneered the use of storyboards as a technique to set the direction of a feature length cartoon, and he designed and directed the development of Disneyland using the storyboard, through which he was able to communicate the essential nature of the kind of theme park he wanted to build.

A key insight behind Disney's remarkable genius was revealed a few days before he died in December of 1966. His last piece of business advice, delivered to a few of his animators from his hospital bed was this, "Get the story. The story's the most important thing. Once you've got the story then everything else will fall into place."

The same thing applies, of course, to storytellers in all media, which include those who create, develop, and manage online brands, for a brand in one important respect is nothing more than a story told to entertain, entice, and engage.

As we saw in Chapter 4, Walt Disney's approach to storytelling became quite influential at Nike, and we adopted storytelling as core business competence throughout product design, branding, and marketing as we developed our brand and the company.

10 | *Ethography*

"*Over time, products and services will come and go, but the brand that provides them remains a constant. Your brand is defined by the sum total of those experiences rather than by the products themselves. The quality of contact builds the relationship out of which emerges our experience of a brand's character. Brand Character can't be communicated proactively. It's earned through behavior and experience over time.*"
– Scott Bedbury, Nike

While the Greek nation of modern times is a small one consisting of only about 11 million people, its culture has exerted a monumental influence on human thought for millennia. As a nation of adept seafarers and traders on the fertile borders between the European, Middle Eastern, and North African cultures, the Greeks were in a unique position to experience a rich variety of ideas, religions, myths, and sciences, and we see how they resulted in a variety of individual, civic, and national outcomes.

While this does not fully explain the Greek genius, it's nevertheless clear that from an historical perspective, a tremendous range of principles, concepts and words come to us from the many generations of Greek scholars whose great works are part of our core values and beliefs even today. And some of these Greek concepts are central to a thorough understanding of brands and branding.

Ethos is the Greek word that means "character," and so it is the study of the guiding beliefs and ideals that characterize a community, ideology, or perhaps even a Fortune 500 enterprise.

The Greeks also used this word to refer to the power of music to influence emotions and behaviors, and thus we extend this concept to refer the power of all media, or any brand touch point, to influence your customer's emotions and behaviors. Ethography is the study of a brand's ethos, its underlying character and influence.

Brand Character analysis is a form of meta-analysis that occurs simultaneously with the seven dimensions of the Brand Field Review that was described in Chapter 8. Those who work inside of a company have a far more intimate understanding of the company's values, beliefs and character than people on the outside, and thus it should be the concern of the brand guardians to extend their senses out to all policies, processes and points of contact that shape the way the company is regarded by the people it is trying to serve, including the people who work there.

For instance, are product returns and defects dealt with swiftly and sincerely? Has the company ever gone beyond basic operations requirements to meet the needs of a customer or employee in crisis? Are there stories of exceptional performance or service on the part of employees or senior executives that have become part of the folklore and character of the company?

These all speak to the internal culture of the brand, as the ideals and exceptional examples become part of the value system of a brand, and its development over time as a force that is precisely intended to have a positive and enduring influence in the market.

Ethnography vs. Ethography

Another important Greek concept is that of ethnos, which refers to culture, and from which we get the discipline of ethnography, the branch of anthropology that is the study of human culture.

In our times, design ethnography has developed into a brilliant tool for navigating the space of human need finding, while its complement brand ethography enables us to navigate meaning and character generated at the brand level. Hence, whereas ethnography deals with understanding product identities, ethography is concerned with brand persona and character that emerge from brand position analysis and from inner field work where the brand guardians group can take imaginative leaps to shape a brand's character in new ways.

Knowing that the market evolves, that consumer tastes evolve, and that important values and meanings in society also evolve, tells us that successful brands must evolve as well. It's simply not reasonable to expect that the brand field defined and developed twenty, ten, or even three years ago will resonate as strongly with the markets and customers of today. Hence, a formal study of brand meaning is essential, and brand ethography and product ethnography are both important tools for doing this work.

Intuition and Rationality

The assumption of rational thinking posits that when people are presented with new information they behave in a logical manner. They (1) think about it, (2) process how they feel about it, and (3) then decide what makes the most sense to do about it.

The assumption that thinking comes first is built into how most commercial advertising is created.

But we all know from direct experience that the reality of how people process information and events in the real world is quite different from this simple one-two-three sequence. Most of us process our feelings first, not our thoughts. We know things first, as we say, "in our gut" and "in our hearts," through our emotional lenses, not our rational ones. We respond first to how things feel intuitively, to the tone in the voice of the speaker, and only later do we consider what they may or may not mean at an intellectual level.

This is in fact how our brains work.

The theory of neurological structure was developed by Dr. Paul MacLean, former director of the Laboratory of the Brain and Behavior at the US National Institute of Mental Health, and it is referred to as the "triune brain theory." MacLean suggests that the human brain is actually three brains in one, each established successively in evolutionary history in response to evolutionary need.

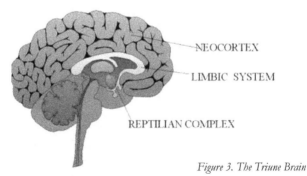

Figure 3. The Triune Brain

The three layers are: the reptilian system of instincts and drives; the limbic system governing emotions and love attachments; and the neocortex, the seat of our logical and rational thinking and our egos. Each performs a separate function, and all three interact.

The reptilian system, or R-complex, consists of the brain stem and the cerebellum. Its purpose is related to physical survival and maintenance of the body, homeostasis. The cerebellum orchestrates movement, digestion, circulation, breathing, execution of the fight or flight response in stress, and reproduction. The R-complex is the brain stem, and plays a crucial role in establishing home territory, mating behaviors and social dominance. The overriding characteristics of R-complex behaviors are that they are automatic, have a ritualistic quality, and are highly resistant to change.

The limbic system evolved later, and is the primary center of emotion. It includes the amygdala, which associates external events with emotion, and the hippocampus, which is active in converting information into long-term memory and in memory recall.

Repeated use of specialized nerve networks in the hippocampus enhances memory storage, so this structure is involved in learning from both commonplace experiences and deliberate study.

Some neuroscientists believe that the hippocampus helps select which memories are stored, perhaps by attaching an "emotion marker" to some events, making them more likely to be recalled. The amygdala comes into play in situations that arouse feelings including fear, pity, anger, or outrage. Damage to the amygdala can abolish an emotion-charged memory.

The limbic system is also involved in primal activities related to food and sex, particularly having to do with our sense of smell and bonding, and activities related to expression and mediation of emotions and feelings of intimacy.

Protective and loving feelings become increasingly complex through connections between the limbic system and the neocortex. The neocortex, also called the cerebral cortex, constitutes nearly 80% of the human brain.

The neocortex makes language, speech, and writing possible, and renders logical and formal operational thinking, allowing us to see ahead and plan for the future. The neocortex also contains two specialized regions, one dedicated to voluntary movement and one to processing sensory information, and it also seems to direct the experience of spirituality.

All three layers of the brain interact because they're inter-connected by an extensive network of nerves. On-going communication between the neocortex and the limbic system links thinking and emotions; each influences the other and both direct all voluntary action. This interplay of memory, emotion, thought and action is the foundation of each person's individuality.

This is all critically important for branding, of course, because these three brains all play a role in the perception of a brand, and brand messaging can be carefully crafted to address the specific attentions of each of these three levels of consciousness.

11 | *Thinking Different*

> *"Your work is going to fill a large part of your life, and the only way to be truly satisfied is to do what you believe is great work. And the only way to do great work is to love what you do. If you haven't found it yet, keep looking. Don't settle. As with all matters of the heart, you'll know when you find it. And, like any great relationship, it just gets better and better as the years roll on. So keep looking until you find it. Don't settle."*
> – Steve Jobs

Douglas McGregor developed his own unique variation on the timeless ideological conflict between fear and love, and articulated it as a management principle, which has been highly influential in the decades since he first published his work, *The Human Side of Enterprise* in 1960.* He recognized that the behavior of managers toward their subordinates often reflects their underlying attitudes towards humanity in general, and he identified two contrasting styles, which he labeled "Theory X" and "Theory Y."

Theory X asserts that humans are fundamentally lazy and must therefore be motivated and controlled. Theory X is based on the assumption that people have no ambition, wish to take no initiative and usually avoid taking any responsibility. To get them to do any work at all, they must be rewarded, coerced, intimidated and punished.

Theory Y suggests that humans are self-motivated and therefore just need to be challenged and channeled to be productive.

---

* Douglas McGregor, *The Human Side of Enterprise*, Annotated Version, McGraw Hill, 2006

Theory X is still the dominant working model in corporate management, and the leaders of many companies still believe that they can achieve their goals by maintaining a certain level of fear in the work force through the threat of lay-offs, and that this leads people to work harder. However, the inherent lack of respect embedded in Theory X creates a negative field dynamic, a downward spiral in human relationship energy resulting from chronically low regard for others.

In one of the most elaborate studies ever done on employee motivation, the Minneapolis Gas Company studied 40,000 employees during a twenty-year period from 1945 to 1965 to determine what they desire most from a job. The study revealed that most considered security, not pay, as the highest rated factor. The next three were opportunity for advancement, the type of work they did, and the desire to work at a company they could be proud of. Hence, financial gain is not the strongest motivator.*

This work helped McGregor in the development of Theory Y, in which he proposed that people prefer the freedom to master challenging work. In this model, a manager's job is to fit the human desire for self-improvement into the organization's need for maximum productive efficiency. Since the basic objectives of both workers and managers are thus fully aligned, with imagination and sincerity enormous potential can be tapped.

Following successful results emanating from experiments to validate Theory Y, psychologist Abraham Maslow developed Theory Z, a humanistic approach with a strong focus on the well being of employees, both on and off the job. Taking these discoveries even further reveals that it's even possible for organizations to tap loving regard as an organizing principle. Doing this requires an enlightened consciousness and positive role modeling from leaders.

Emotional Intelligence

Reflecting this possibility, Daniel Goleman's extensive research in the broad field of managerial self-awareness has resulted in two brilliant best selling books, *Emotional Intelligence*† and *Working with Emotional Intelligence*‡, in which Goleman focuses upon why and how some senior executives succeed while others fail.

In Goleman's terms, emotional intelligence comprises five core competencies:

---

* The Minneapolis Gas Company study can be found at www.bpir.com

† Emotional Intelligence by Daniel Goleman, Bantam, 2006

‡ Working with Emotional Intelligence by Daniel Goleman, Bantam, 1998

- Self-Awareness: the ability to recognize and understand your own moods, emotions and drives.
- Self-Regulation: the ability to control or redirect disruptive impulses and moods, and the propensity to suspend judgment – to think before acting.
- Motivation: a passion for work, for reasons that go beyond money or status.
- Empathy: the ability to understand the emotional make-up, needs, and attitudes of other people.
- Social Skill: proficiency in managing relationships and building networks, and an ability to find the common ground and build rapport.

These insights can be put to work in organizations through hiring practices, as well as human resources development and even in succession management. Thus, does your company interview prospective job candidates with these criteria in mind? Does your company endeavor to develop these traits in its employees? Does your organization identify and select future leaders on the basis of these human skills?

These are all critical leadership skills that relate to soulful brand development. They are not technical or vocational skills; they are personality or character traits that can be nurtured and developed with the right kind of mentors and models present in childhood and education.

Of course every corporate leader is wired a little differently. If the top leaders of your organization lack some of these personality traits, then pursuing a soulful brand strategy may not be right for your brand. The development of intangible value in human relationships and brand relationships absolutely requires the presence of these personality traits.

Inspiring Customers to Think Different

Walter Isaacson's biography of Steve Jobs exposes two quite different aspects of Jobs' personality and his management style. At times he could be very hard on people, but he also had a skill, like Walt Disney, for inspiring people to do their best work, evoking performances that may have been otherwise unattainable.

This is often the case with great leaders, who are often fascinating characters to study because they are full of paradoxes and contradictions. We know from his legacy at Apple that he had a deeply soulful side, which is evident in this story:

When Jobs returned to Apple in 1997, he found that the Apple brand had gone through a long period of neglect and was in need of renewal. He lamented the fact that Apple had drifted from its founding values, as its marketing had followed an old and tired product positioning formula used by other technology firms that extolled the virtues of "our product" versus "their product."

He knew that the way back was not in talking about why Apple's User Interface was better than Windows, or why Apple's processors were faster. Instead, he saw that the marketing challenge was to give the brand more heart and soul. Jobs realized that if Apple were to become great again, it needed an inspirational brand story. This is how Steve explained his understanding of Apple's brand challenge shortly after returning to Apple after his ten-year absence:

"Marketing is about values. This is a very complicated and noisy world. And we're not going to get a chance for people to remember much about us. No company is. So we have to be really clear on what we want them to know about us. Now Apple fortunately is one of the half a dozen best brands in the whole world, right up there with Nike, Disney, Coke and Sony. It is one of the greats of the greats, not just in this country but all around the globe. But even a great brand needs investment and caring if it's going to maintain its relevance and vitality. The Apple brand has clearly suffered from neglect. We need to bring it back. The way to do that is not to talk about speeds and feeds. It's not to talk about MIPS and megahertz. It's not to talk about why we're better than Windows.

The best example of all and one of the best jobs of marketing the universe has ever seen is Nike. Nike sells a commodity. They sell shoes. And yet when you think of Nike, you think of something different than just a shoe company. In their ads they don't ever talk about the product. They don't ever talk about their air soles and why they are better than Reebok's air soles. What does Nike do in their advertising? They honor great athletes, and they honor great athletics. That's who they are. That's what they are all about.

Apple spends a fortune on advertising. But you'd never know it. So, when I got here Apple had just fired its agency, and there was a competition between 20 ad agencies to win the business in maybe four years. So I blew that up. And we hired Chiat Day. We started working a few weeks ago with Chiat Day, and we learned that our customers want to know, 'Who Is Apple? What is it that Apple stands for?'

What Apple is about isn't making boxes for people to get their jobs done, although we do that well. We do that better than almost everybody in some cases. But Apple is about something more than that. Apple at the core, its core value … is that, we believe that people with passion can change the world for the better. That's what we believe. And we believe that in this world people can change it for the better. And that those people who are crazy enough to think they can change the world, are the ones that do.

And so what we're going to do in the first major brand marketing campaign in a number *of years is to get back to that core value. The things that Apple believed in at its core are the same things that Apple believes in today. And so we wanted to find a way to communicate this. What we have is something that I am very moved by. It honors those people who have changed the world. Some of them are living and some of them are not. But, the ones that aren't as you'll see, you know that if they'd ever used a computer it would have been a Mac. The theme of this campaign is 'Think Different.' It honors the people who think different and who move this world forward."* *

Apple's profoundly successful and influential Think Different campaign emerged from an internal brand purpose review to locate and project the core values of the brand. It was an expression of the genius latent in the Apple brand, and an enduring example of iconic, empathic and soulful branding.

Think Different projected heart and soul into a category where those energies were almost completely absent, and directly attached those positive energies to the Apple brand. It then stood out against the industry backdrop of product positioning ads, and said something important about what Apple as a brand stood for. It spoke directly to the identities of the people it was striving to reach.

And most importantly, the tone of the campaign was delivered in such a way that it struck an emotional chord. The campaign generated an elevated feeling about the nature of genius, the nature of Apple's genius, and about the genius of people who buy Apple computers to do creative things with a certain kind of spirit, intention, and style. It was itself an act of genius to align all these things and to also push the internal culture of the company forward in the process. This is an excellent example of a deep campaign and how such a campaign can successfully communicate on multiple levels at the same time.

---

*   Steve Jobs, September 23, 1997: https://www.youtube.com/watch?v=9GMQhOm-Dqo

12 | *Depth Campaigns*

"Transforming a brand into a socially responsible leader doesn't happen overnight by simply writing new marketing and advertising strategies. It takes effort to identify a vision that your customers will find credible and aligned with their values."
— Simon Mainwaring

With the understanding of a cultural ethos clearly defined, a creative team seeks to leverage ideas linked to a brand's essence, attaching unique, strong and favorable brand associations and energies that enable it to stand out, to say something important that resonates emotionally and intellectually, to connect with human inspiration, aspiration, and dreams.

It's obvious that the underlying energy of a depth campaign is very different from conventional product advertising, which commonly plays upon insecurity or superficiality. Depth campaigns find something to celebrate that shows the genius and vitality of living life on a more soulful level.

From Think Different to Just Do It

Apple's Think Different is an example of a "deep campaign," one that leverages cultural truths and aspirations, and which attempts to unify the ethos of the culture with the ethos of a brand.

In a 1994 interview for PBS that aired as the 'One Last Thing' documentary, Steve Jobs commented:

"When you grow up you tend to get told the world is the way it is and your life is just to live your life inside the world. Try not to bash into the walls too much. Try to have a nice family life, have fun, save a little money. That's a very limited life. Life can be much broader once you discover one simple fact, and that is – everything around you that you call life, was made up by people that were no smarter than you. And you can change it, you can influence it, you can build your own things that other people can use. The minute that you understand that you can poke life and actually something will pop out the other side, that you can change it, you can mold it. That's maybe the most important thing. It's to shake off this erroneous notion that life is there and you're just gonna live in it, versus embrace it, change it, improve it, make your mark upon it. I think that's very important, and however you learn that, once you learn it, you'll want to change life and make it better, cause it's kind of messed up, in a lot of ways. Once you learn that, you'll never be the same again."

From these comments it's not so difficult to see where the inspiration for Apple's 1997 Think Different campaign originated.

At Nike, ten years earlier than *Think Different*, Scott Bedbury was hired as head of global advertising. This was in the midst of our discovery that the Nike brand was speaking only to a very narrow range of extreme male athletes, and that we needed to become relevant to wider circles of people, including women and baby boomer males who were active in fitness pursuits but not in competitive sports. We recognized that Nike had an opportunity to become the protagonist of all that was great and uplifting about the actual experience of participating in these activities.

However, Nike's ad agency was producing ads at that time with elite athletes in pro sports performance situations, largely ignoring the much larger groups who were participating in various sports and fitness movements. The running, aerobics and fitness movements engaged more than 150 million people, while pro and college sports involved about 1 million in total. Based on these insights, Scott presented a one page brief to Nike's agency W+K:

"Nike is about to become a significant network television advertiser. We will spend nearly three times what we spent on the *Revolution* campaign in the fall of 1988. (Despite the high visibility of *Revolution*, Nike had spent less than $5 million on TV that year). This is a turning point for a company that not long ago spoke to its customers at track meets from the tailgate of a station wagon. This just cannot be a narrow look back at where we have been. We should be proud of our heritage, but we must also realize that the appeal of *Hayward Field* (an ad recently produced, set at the University of Oregon's track & field stadium) is narrow and potentially alienating to those who are not great athletes. We need to grow this brand beyond its purest core ... we have to stop talking just to ourselves. It's time to widen the access point. We need to capture a more complete spectrum of the rewards of sports and fitness. We achieved this with *Revolution*. Now we need to take the next step."[*]

W+K came back to Nike two weeks later with storyboards for a new campaign, for which agency co-founder Dan Wieden had come up with a compelling new tagline: *Just Do It.*

The campaign captured the spirit of the emerging fitness movements and the hidden spirit at the core of Nike and spoke to both genders and to people young and old about putting off procrastination and excuses and getting active. The campaign captured something uplifting about the human spirit, and channeled it through the Nike brand.

W+K used the tag line with dozens of creative executions across a range of sports in a deep campaign concept that has endured for 25 years, becoming the anthem for the Nike brand, which for decades created one unifying theme. The tagline became a meme in social conversations long before the Internet took off, and created hundreds of millions of positive associations for the brand.

The campaign also resonated within the internal culture of Nike, supporting and encouraging people to work out during lunchtime. About half the workforce went on a run or went to the company-provided gym, so the *Just Do It* tagline captured the DNA of the brand through its employees' own daily experiences.

Prior to *Just Do It*, Nike was primarily a quirky, niche defined, national brand. After *Just Do It*, Nike became known as a global marketing powerhouse, and quickly developed into one of the premier brands in the world.

Great campaigns are memorable and meaningful, and they resonate by connecting the brand or product with the way people actually live their lives. *Just Do It* and *Think Different* accomplished all these things, and they also regenerated the brand character, soul and vitality for both Apple and Nike in a time of extreme adversity for both companies.

Nike has located another sweet spot with its *Find Your Greatness* campaign, which has touched a great many people because once again it's such a positive and inclusive message that inspires everyone. This is what depth campaigns do.

The Beats by Dr. Dre, *Hear What You Want* is also an ingenious campaign that shows how professional athletes sustain their focus with the help of a

---

[*] Scott Bedbury: A New Brand World, Viking, 2002, p 38

headset, a message everyone can identify with: *overcome critics and self-doubt to go forward and succeed.*

The Value of a Strong Brand Reputation

Depth campaigns are a critical element that contributes to the development of a strong and vibrant brand, and when such campaigns are well designed and well implemented, the results can be very significant not only for the marketing effort, but for the broader organization as well. This happens because the value of any company is more and more linked with the value of its brands.

With the dawn of the Age of Intellectual Capital during the 1990s came the realization that much of the real wealth in the modern enterprise resides in the intangible assets, and not in traditional tangible assets such as real estate, plant, equipment, inventory, or cash.

To understand the importance of intangible assets we need only look at the market capitalization of many of today's most successful corporations, or at the prices paid beyond conventional asset values in recent mergers and acquisitions.

At the end of February 2015, with a market capitalization of $750 billion, Apple reported revenues for FY 2014 of $183 billion. If we check its balance sheet, and add its stated conventional assets of $232 billion to its annual revenues, we are still left with $335 billion worth of market cap of unspecified value. What accounts for this $335 billion? Experts agree this represents Apple's intangible assets, or intellectual capital, of which, according to Forbes, $124 billion is the Apple brand.*

The intangible assets in some successful organizations are worth more than their physical or book assets.

The market research industry has devised a half dozen ways of calculating brand equity. Elements that can be included in brand equity valuation include market share, market share growth rate, profit margins, aided and unaided brand awareness levels, recognition of logos and other visual elements, brand language associations made by consumers, consumers' perceptions of quality, and other relevant brand values.

Brand equity can be created through strategic investments in advertising and in communications channels, and in market education. For example, Apple has educated the public about the Apple brand by opening its own retail stores, which showcase the brand in the most positive light and assist custom-

---

* Forbes 2014 List of the Worlds 100 Most Valuable Brands – http://www.forbes.com/powerful-brands/

ers with technical questions and service issues to get fast and easy answers through the Genius Bar.

Brand equity appreciates through the growth of a company, and contributes to the growth of profit margins, market share, prestige value and the integrated value when product families work together, as Apple has achieved through its unified product set that includes iMac, iPod, iPad, iCloud, iTunes, iPhone, and the App Store. Insightful strategic investments that add new layers of integrated value connected to a positive brand purpose help a company's market capitalization accrete greater value over time.

While brand equity is strategically crucial, it has been famously difficult to quantify. Many experts have developed tools to analyze it, but there is still today no agreed upon standard way to measure it, and at least six alternatives are widely in use: the Aaker Model, Moran Model, Young & Rubicam Model, Interbrand Model, CoreBrand Model, Conjoint Analysis model. Our point here is not to analyze them or identify one above the others, but merely to point out that this is still an evolving field of study.

One of the common challenges that marketing professionals and academics find with the concept of brand equity is a disconnect between quantitative and qualitative equity values. Quantitative calculations include numerical values such as profit margin and market share, but fail to capture qualitative elements such as prestige value and other key brand associations of consumer interest like product and communications resonance.

Regardless of the model used, the brand equity calculation conundrum points to the fact that intangible qualities in marketing result in the creation of tangible qualities on the balance sheet, which then become most apparent when a company is sold. Considering this, we can see why "the Brand" has moved to the center of corporate strategy and why it is one of the most valuable assets in the enterprise and a primary strategic asset for both competitive strategy and sustainable competitive advantage.

As business leaders realize the large role that strategic brand protection, development and management can play, the business planning paradigm can shift as the brand, which was once thought of as the concern of the VP of Marketing, now becomes the ongoing concern of the entire executive team and all employees whose jobs touch the public.

If you don't know what your brand really stands for, or if you are not developing more soulful qualities in your brand field, then you simply haven't yet positioned your company or your brand in a way that will enable its greatest success.

The deep campaign is perhaps the best example of a brand development strategy that strives for locating the brand purpose and then amplifying it in such a way that allows all people connected to the brand to celebrate some aspect about what life and living are really all about.

13 | *Mindfulness*

"When we are mindful, deeply in touch with the present moment, our understanding of what is going on deepens, and we begin to be filled with acceptance, joy, peace and love."
— Thich Nhat Hanh

Being fully present means that we engage our whole selves in whatever it is that we are doing. Our attention, our intentions, our thoughts, our feelings and our energy are focused in the present moment, and on the tasks at hand.

Being present is a powerful experience, and when we are in this state we feel completely alive and invigorated.

This sense of aliveness is natural when we are absorbed in work or play that we love, and it is available to us in every moment because we can learn to summon it regardless of what we are doing. Even tasks or jobs we don't enjoy can become infused with the light of being present.

Here and Now

Researchers at the University of California at Santa Barbara found that college students who were trained in mindfulness performed better on the verbal reasoning section of college exams, and also experienced improvements in their working memories. UCSB scientist Michael Mrazek notes, "Our results suggest that cultivating mindfulness is an effective and efficient technique for improving cognitive function, with wide reaching consequences."*

At the Institute for Psychological Research and Leiden Institute for Brain and Cognition of Leiden University in the Netherlands, researchers also found tremendous impact of mindfulness on creativity. Dr. Lorenza Colzato sum-

---

* Michael Mrazek, 2013, Psychological Science 24(5) 776-781

marized, "Mindfulness meditation induces a control state that promotes divergent thinking, a style of thinking that allows many new ideas to be generated." Being fully present thus may help you to produce more ideas and better quality ideas.

Another study* showed that meditation practice reduces cognitive rigidity. In the experiment, subjects were given six tasks, the first three of which required complex solutions, and the last three progressively easier ones. Non-meditators continued to apply the difficult solution methods to the easy problems, and were more likely to become frustrated. Meditators were more likely to quickly figure out that the later problems could be solved using fewer and easier steps.

The authors concluded that mindfulness meditation reduced the tendency to be "blinded" by experience. In other words, being fully present reduces the tendency to reinforce blind spots that prevent you from seeing novel and adaptive ways to solve problems, or to even see that a problem exists. The meditators were less rigid in their thinking, and they ruminated less about failures.

Mindfulness in the Corporate Environment

For all of these reasons, many companies have started meditation classes for their employees. Ray Dalio, the head of one of the world's biggest hedge funds, Bridgewater Associates, with about $150 billion in assets, explains that his own meditation practice has helped his investment management performance. He says, "Meditation more than anything in my life was the biggest ingredient for whatever success I've had. It gives me a centeredness, it gives me an ability to look at things without the emotional hijacking, without the ego, in a way that gives me a certain clarity."†

Leaders at many other companies have reached the same conclusion. Google offers a mindfulness course called "Search Inside Yourself," and more than a thousand employees have participated in it.‡ The Google campus also offers a labyrinth for walking meditation.

EBay offers meditation rooms equipped with pillows and flowers, and Evan Williams, a co-founder of Twitter, has introduced regular meditation sessions in his new venture, the Obvious Corporation, a start-up incubator

---

* "Mind the Trap": Mindfulness Practice Reduces Cognitive Rigidity, Published 5/15/12, PLOS One, Jonathan Greenberg, Keren Reiner, Nachshon Meiran

† Tradermind, by Steve Ward, 2015, John Wiley & Sons

‡ The Mindfulness Revolution, Edited by Barry Boyce, Shambala Publications, 2011

and investment vehicle.*

General Mills deputy general counsel Janice Marturano, who founded a mindfulness program, noted, "It's about training our minds to be more focused, to see with clarity, to have spaciousness for creativity and to feel connected. That compassion to ourselves, to everyone around us – our colleagues, customers – that's what the training of mindfulness is really about."†

Nike has created a play sanctuary on its corporate campus, with state-of-the-art sports and fitness facilities on 200 wooded acres, and has found that these facilities generate a tremendous productivity and creativity boost by allowing people to re-charge and interact in a playful way during the workday. Informal, ad hoc interactions spark new ideas and inspire more work to get done, and people who would not normally meet, gather to network and have productive discussions. Not coincidentally, Nike doesn't target and segment consumers by demographics; instead it studies and identifies behaviors and psychographics around "fields of play."

Mindfulness and Branding

Being fully present is also at the core of soulful branding. As it is where we experience aliveness and genius, it is central to the learning that we must engage in to develop brands that are fully aligned with the mind of the market, with the deeper spirit of intuitive response and resonance that we seek.

Engaging with customers in a fully present way allows you to tap into emotions and feelings, and to understand them as they are, rather than merely as statistics, personas, abstractions or numerical profiles.

Empathy is the core sensing ability and skill of both etho-graphy and ethno-graphy.

Empathy

Mindfulness also transforms one's ability to see, think and feel from another's perspective, that is, to empathize. Empathy is the ability to sense others' emotions and is one of the most important ingredients in developing meaningful relationships. This can be a hard mode of perception to tune into for executives who feel time starved, burdened with too many tasks, or who are working under extreme pressure, or in fear-driven situations.

Emotions are rarely verbalized but are usually communicated through the tone of voice, shift in posture, gesture and facial expressions. When we are

---

* The Mindfulness Business, The Economist, 11/16/13, Schumpeter, p92

† http://www.theconsciousprofessional.com/library/articles/invest-in-meditation

fully present we will not only be able to see deeper insights and get better ideas, but our customers may sense our aliveness and regard for them, strengthening the energy and information exchange on the interactive field.

The concept of empathy encompasses a broad range of emotional states, including caring for other people and having a desire to help them, experiencing emotions that match another person's emotions, discerning what another person is thinking or feeling, and making less distinct the differences between the self and the other. It also is the ability to feel and share another person's emotions.

Empathy involves the ability to match another's emotions, and being tenderhearted toward others. The ability to experience empathy is also absolutely essential for depth researchers to understand and directly experience emotional energy on the interactive brand field. The ability to understand other people – what motivates them and how to work with them – is a large part of interpersonal intelligence, which correlates with intrapersonal intelligence, the ability to form a realistic model of oneself.

In the field of positive psychology, empathy has also been compared and contrasted with altruism and egotism. Altruism is behavior that is aimed at benefitting another person, while egotism is a behavior that is acted out for personal gain.*

The ability to imagine oneself as another person is a sophisticated imaginative process, but the basic capacity to recognize emotions is probably innate and may be achieved unconsciously.39†

Empathy on behalf of the brand leaders in regard to the people they intend to serve is the hidden driver behind the creation of Soulful Brands. This insight can easily be lost or overlooked. There are plenty of other more direct economic imperatives that vie for one's business attention. The reason it is overlooked, ironically, is that "empathy" is not initially sensed with the intellect, but instead with the feeling function that we all possess when we process consciousness through our hearts.

Consciousness can be sourced from many different locations inside of human experience. For anyone with a college education, because of the rigorous demands placed upon the intellect to graduate, consciousness is primarily

---

* [Snyder, C. R., Shane J. Lopez, and Jennifer T. Pedrotti. Positive Psychology: The Scientific and Practical Explorations of Human Strengths

† Happiness Genes: Unlock the Positive Potential Hidden in Your DNA, New Page Books (April, 2010)] It can also be trained and achieved. [O'Malley W. J. (1999). "Teaching Empathy". America 180 (12): 22–26

sourced from the head, rational thinking and egoistic thinking. To shift to an empathetic point of view is to listen and participate from one's heart.

Throughout this book we've shared different perspectives and questions to get you to shift your mode of perception when viewing everyday challenges and problems. If you can learn to make this shift in your planning exercises and execute new brand initiatives that truly resonate with people inside and outside of your company, then you'll have learned one of the most important lessons in Soulful Branding.

14 | *Dream Catching at Starbucks*

"If you can dream it, you can do it."
— Walt Disney

"If you have built castles in the air, your work need not be lost; that is where they should be. Now put foundations under them."
— Henry David Thoreau

Starbucks was established in 1971, but the extraordinary success of the company is built upon nearly eight hundred years of fascinating history. For legend has it that coffee was discovered in Ethiopia more than 800 years ago, when a goat herder noted that his goats became much friskier after eating a particular type of red berries. One thing led to another, and soon coffee beans were being exported from Ethiopia to Yemen, and then throughout the Mideast and on to Europe. The word coffee itself is derived from an Arabic word, which we translate as "wine of the bean."

The first coffeehouse known to history opened in Constantinople in 1554, and legend also has it that soldiers of the Polish-Hapsburg army, while liberating Vienna from the second Turkish siege in 1683, found a number of sacks with strange beans that they initially thought were camel feed. They intended to burn it, but the Polish king granted the sacks to one of his officers, who then opened the first coffee house in Europe.

Over the next century, coffee houses opened up all over Europe, and perhaps it can even be credited with changing the consciousness of Europeans on a large scale. For prior to the widespread consumption of coffee people typically consumed vast quantities of wine and beer, drinking pretty much all day long, largely because in most cities the water was considered unsafe to drink. In employee records of the time, the specific quantity of mead, beer, ale, or wine was specified in detail, and the quantities were not modest.

As you can imagine, there wasn't much productive work going on by the end of the day. How much we can credit coffee with the Enlightenment and the Industrial Revolution is hard to say, but it is clear that productivity did improve dramatically as alcohol consumption declined (and the expanding understanding of science and machinery surely helped also).

Fast-forward a few hundred years to 1996, and Jerome Conlon has just joined Starbucks to help develop the company's brand identity. CEO Howard Schultz was concerned that Starbucks would not achieve its potential as a brand if it merely imitated the strategies of McDonalds and other fast food companies, so the internal brand group and the retail store design team were instructed to work together to think out-of-the-quick-service-restaurant-box, and to develop a vision of the coffee house of the future.

The team focused on this question: How could the inherent soulful qualities of coffee be better reflected in Starbucks retail stores? The depth research process Jerome put in place to answer this question was coined by Scott Bedbury as *The Big Dig*. This process resembled an archeological dig to uncover the history of coffee in the world and how this history was affecting the mindset of the marketplace for coffee around the globe in 1996.

At the time, the company was opening new locations at a rate of more than one per day, so there was already a massive design, planning, logistics, and capital investment effort under way.

And yet there was at the same time a nagging feeling among the company's leaders that they could be doing it better. But it was difficult to put their finger precisely on what should be improved, so over the following six months Jerome and his team performed a psychological dig through the history, ethos, and culture of coffee using a mixture of some of the brand scanning techniques described in the previous chapters, and by doing research on the history of coffee and coffee houses from their origins.

Consumer depth workshops were also held in many cities across America, with participants including men and women, young and old, working people and students; one of the discovery techniques we used was a projection exercise around the nature of the ideal coffee shop, which Jerome called "dream catching."

Through dream catching the participants were able to delve into the power of a dream state as a means of conceiving of and designing ideal experiences.

They closed their eyes and imagined that they were enjoying the best cup of coffee they'd ever had, in the best coffee shop they had ever been. Through a group meditation and guided visualization they were quietly encouraged to notice the other people in the cafe, what the space looked like, the plants, furniture, lighting, colors and textures, the smells, the sounds, and the food.

When the mediation period ended the participants were asked to describe what they had seen, and surprisingly their descriptions were all very similar. It was as if they'd all read the same book, or watched the same movie.

This, we discovered, was the shared romantic ideal, which the artistic and soulful coffee house represents, a nearly universal vision shared so consistently across ages, genders, geography and demographics. Thus, the ideal coffee shop, as it turns out, is an archetype in the collective subconscious. The resulting imagery helped us to close the gap between what Starbucks had started to become in the public eye, a corporate coffee chain, and the much more ideal experience of an iconic soulful coffee house that so many respondents had visualized.

These "Ideal Coffee House" research findings were then translated into a store design brief, highlighting the visual cues and design codes that Starbucks designers needed to pay attention to. Wright Massey, Starbucks head of design and former head of Disney retail store design, embraced these insights. Wright started the design phenomenon in America of "retail as entertainment" with the design of the first Disney retail store in the Glendale Galleria mall.

Armed with these insights, the Starbucks store design team found new ways to bring the history and mythology of coffee to life in new ways, not just in the design of the stores, but also in packaging, posters, promotions, print advertising, the employee handbook and even in the Starbucks Annual Report.

A unique symbol and packaging style was developed for each variety of coffee, and a story was crafted to explain the stages needed to produce the perfect cup of coffee. The team also developed symbols and graphics to go with each major holiday, and highly stylized but low cost wall murals turned blank walls into rich stories and imagery.

It should be noted that all of the above integrated design tasks were not originally part of the retail store design group's charter. These additional design tasks grew organically out of their skills and vision for what the brand could become. And in this sense this group evolved into one of the first in-house brand development studios capable of taking on almost any creative task.

The retail store design group was also given the task of reimagining not just a single store concept but four distinctly different store concepts that all drew from a common kit of parts, both functional and artistic, which reduced the cost of building out new stores by 22%. As this work was going on, a group of Wall Street analysts were invited to tour Starbucks headquarters where they saw the full-scale models of the new store prototypes and the incredible creative output of this brand development studio at work. The next morning when their reports hit the media, Starbucks share price jumped by about 20%.

Sharing the Vision

But it was not enough for the ideal Starbucks coffee shop vision to be expressed only through design. It also had to be expressed through behavior, through each and every Starbucks employee at each location. Hence, we had to reach into the entire organization to share the vision.

One of the first venues where this was attempted was at a convention of Starbucks store managers.

Research had revealed that in the public mind, the Starbucks brand was starting to lose its soul and was even becoming like "the McDonalds of coffee," so Deepak Chopra had been invited to speak to the group about the human soul, hoping to help hundreds of managers reconnect with a deeper understanding of what soul was, and why it mattered to Starbucks. Deepak's talk was a moving experience, and helped to evoke the depth and nuance that moved the group far beyond the superficial platitudes that are common in corporate management meetings.

Jerome spoke next and delivered a presentation on the topic of brand soul, focusing on his perceptions about what business Starbucks was really in. Some believed that Starbucks was in the coffee business, others that it was the quick-service restaurant business, and others still, that it was the packaged goods business.

Our research, of course, had taught us that the real opportunity was to position the brand in alignment with the consumer experience we were striving to create inside the coffee shop itself. The brand field energy integrated music, the colors and lighting, the friendliness of the people, with the various types of furniture to create a compelling mood in which the beverages and food fit naturally and inseparably into one iconic and archetypical café experience. So this was the brand vision we shared, an inspirational story and perspective on the ideal coffee shop archetype that the company was looking for, a cause and a purpose that would set the Starbucks brand apart.

It worked, as you know, and the company continued to extend this work in the coming years. As Starbucks exemplified the coffee house archetype, it also gained permission in the mind of the public to extend it and indeed to play with it, giving it a uniquely American twist while remaining true to the brand's own set of values. Hence, connecting the soul of the Starbucks brand with the deeper history and meaning of coffee and the coffee house contributed to the company's rapid growth and development in the following decade as it grew beyond its American roots and established itself as a global brand, one that continued to evolve and develop.

15 | *The Evolving Brand: Air Jordan*

"Learn to love change. Feel comfortable with your own creative intuition. Make compassion, care, harmony, and trust the foundation stones of business. Fall in love with new ideas."
– Anita Roddick, Founder of The Body Shop

Michael Jordan's stunning tomahawk dunk, captured in the iconic photograph taken during a college playoff game, suggested in a single image the Air Jordan character long before Jordan had ever worn a pair of Nike shoes. This "Jumpman" image, as it would later be called, was the potent visual seed that led to the birth of the most successful character marketing campaign in the history of sports.

Even today, more than a dozen years since he last played in the NBA, about 58% of all basketball shoes sold in the US are still Air Jordans. The brand generates more than $2.5 billion in annual sales, and based largely on this success, Michael Jordan's personal net worth recently surpassed $1 billion. He earns $80 to $100 million in endorsements annually.

How is it that the brand has stayed vibrant even as the unique athlete around whom the brand is oriented is more than a decade beyond his playing days?

This highlights the fact that successful brands are not just static. Instead, their meaning evolves and they take on different forms as the knowledge and spirit within a company and its products grows and unfolds, and as the mind of the market evolves in response to the full range of external factors and conditions.

In the same way, Apple's 'Think Different' campaign wasn't just about the Apple brand values, it was also about the values its consumers embodied and admired as well. Advertising agency Chiat Day found a way to align the internal equities of the Apple brand with aspirational character traits of Apple consumers, enabling Apple to embody and communicate the ideal values that its artistic, creative and rebellious customers deeply identified with.

Air Jordan as a product, and Think Different as a campaign, both achieved the pinnacle of branding success, rising to the status of icons.

And obviously, to take branding to the iconic level it's not enough to be merely inventive or clever. You have to understand the meaning of the brand at a deeper level, to deconstruct it and re-perceive it over and over, perhaps like a composer striving to perfect a symphony. What role does the brand play in peoples' lives? What are the mythological or archetypal themes that resonate most deeply? What is the ideal? And how do ideals translate into product design codes?

As Douglas Holt tells us, "An iconic brand is a person, company or trademark that is widely regarded as the most compelling symbol of what it represents. It embodies a set of ideals or values that society deems has important 'identity value.' Iconic brands find ways to 'author' stories that perform identity myths … the right identity myth well performed provides the audience with little epiphanies - moments of recognition that put feelings on barely perceptible desires."

Because a brand serves as a modern talisman it must reflect a core archetype relating to human meaning and motivation.

Michael Jordan tapped into the sports warrior archetype, his battlefield the hyper- competitive arena of the NBA, where he demonstrated never-before seen athletic skills. He had cat-like quickness that could freeze the best defenders, and a style that made him look like a speedboat in a sea of battleships, and his incredible four foot vertical leap put the top of his head 6 inches above the rim.

And while the Air Jordan phenomenon was built on his talent, the iconic quality of the brand was largely a reflection of his personality, his undeniable charisma and magnetism. The challenge for Nike was to capture Jordan's unique character in a shoe, and to understand and develop this aspect of the brand. A critical skill in this process was the translation of Jordan's personal character into product design codes. Nike's Senior Vice President of Design and Special Projects, Tinker Hatfield took on the design translation process. Like Disney, Hatfield began using storyboards to visually think his way through the evolution of a product or project concept. Tinker liked to tell a story about the design inspiration behind a new shoe and link it to Jordan's character, playing style and personality.

A character like Jordan that embodies a brand story, like the Nike brand itself, does not exist in a vacuum. It exists in the same field as the one in which the brand operates, and thus the space surrounding a character's life needs to be explored and developed. Factors such as cultural influences, family, ethnic background, social class, religious background, educational background, location, and occupation are all part what makes any given person unique, and this context has huge influence on a character's speech, movement, attitude and behaviors, largely defining what is credible and real for a character to say and do. And to these culture codes Hatfield also looked deeply into MJ's playing style, on-court antics, off-court dress and sense of style. These factors too were fair game for being interpreted and translated into design codes that were then embedded in the Air Jordan products.

Hatfield used this character study technique in the pairing of Mighty Mouse and Bo Jackson in the design of one of the first true Cross Training shoes, and when he developed a design for Air Jordan shoe from the nose art painted on a WWII-era British Spitfire fighter plane. This flaming nose art became the image embedded in the mid-sole of the Air Jordan 5.

Jordan's interest in collecting and racing exotic, high performance motorcycles become another source of design inspiration. Finding inspiration from motorcycle tires, Tinker created the signature shoe that celebrated the twenty-year history of Air Jordan. Embedded in the mesh of the heels were the numbers 85 and 05, and the lace covers were laser etched with symbols representing different stages in the life of Michael Jordan.

This attention to design codes in the Jordan shoes, which occurred throughout the evolution of the Air Jordan brand, was definitely noticed on the street, and it helped to fuel a passion for the product that endures to this day. Through this process, Nike's designers learned that a brand could be built upon the emotional life of a character both inside and outside the game by translating them into design elements, features, codes and even attitudes.

Brand characters who are infused with their own emotional lives, with specific attitudes and values, will become multi-dimensional, authentic characters rather than cookie cutter copies or shallow, 2-D cardboard clichés. These details come through when designers and researchers observe the unique ways that people do things, their distinguishing characteristics, and the small details that make them singular and special. These can be actions, behaviors, figures of speech, gestures or an unusual approach that your character takes to a particular situation.

Details can also be expressed and highlighted through a character's imperfections, not just from positive attributes. A perfect character with no flaws or human weakness is commonly perceived by an audience as being boring, uninteresting and unreal or inhuman. Authentic characters in the real world are full of paradoxes and contradictions, and through storytelling it is these imperfections, how they are revealed and how they are overcome that draws the audience's interest and creates a rooting interest.

Flaws, in other words, may be inherently valuable, and among the earliest artists to formally appreciate the irregular character of beauty were the tea masters of Japan. The bowls used in their tea ceremony often show some form of irregularity. The shapes are often irregular, the surfaces dry or sandy, the glazes of uneven thickness where the pieces were piled in the kiln and remained unglazed where pots rested upon one another. Cracks were accepted. Characteristics and flaws such as these were not merely tolerated, they were taken as integral to clay pot making, and contributed to a pot's beauty, for depth of character exists precisely in the natural imperfections. Hence, the tea masters' pursuit of profound natural truth led them to reject the perfect for the imperfect, reject the overly precise because it negated the overtones in nature, and thus admitted no freedom. The perfect translated into a design form was seen as too often static and regulated, too cold, and hard.

Appreciation of character imperfections is also central to the appeal of movies and TV stories in which characters evolve and develop over the course of a season. Audiences are interested in the emotional lives of the characters they appreciate, their fears, joys, and vulnerabilities, and observing these qualities opens a character to the audience in a form of intimacy that makes storytelling through books or filmed entertainment so compelling.

Great performers are great not just because of their great physical beauty, but because of great depth of character that they reveal in the roles they play, and their capacity to embody a character's flaws, express them, and learn from them so that both the actor and the audience grow in understanding and in spirit.

Just as an author performs backstory research into the characters they write about, planning the development of a brand's character is thus essential to the creation of a robust brand character. And it involves similar skills in researching and imagining what values and motives guide the brand's character, and how might this character evolve over time as it struggles with imperfections.

Characters also exist in relationships. Most character driven stories embody interactions between people in small groups, paired up as partners including friends, lovers, buddies, cops, and married couples, and in small ensembles such as we saw in Seinfeld and Friends. These ensembles allow the writers and actors to explore an unlimited world of story dynamics involving personal chemistry and personality quirks, preferences, and anomalies that make other characters in the group go crazy, and which are rich sources of endless humor and insight.

Relational character stories emphasize the chemistry between characters, while brand stories used in advertising commonly rely on conflict or competition to provide tension and drama which is then resolved in some kind of issue or problem that reveals the brand as the solution. Much more infrequent, but much more powerful, is brand storytelling that results in the transformation of a character who learns something vital and new, and in which the brand itself plays a catalytic role.

And of course this is one of the reasons that the Nike and Apple brands have been prominently featured here. Both went through a period in their marketing histories when they were product oriented in their positioning, and both grew to become transcendental by enlarging their vision and scope beyond the product to become life enhancing and iconic as enablers.

So while a product focuses on physical features and compares one product with others, or talks about physical features and the physical benefits, more powerful and less frequent is storytelling that places a product in a realistic context that shows how it is experienced and how it transforms ordinary moments into extraordinary ones.

Brand Facets

Some experts will tell you that a brand should present a consistent identity and should not change, at the risk of losing its loyal franchise. The risk, however, is that after a period of minor incremental changes the brand will become increasingly irrelevant, and this kind of a static approach ends in the need to radically reposition the brand to catch up with a fast moving, dynamic and competitive marketplace.

Just as people and institutions grow and develop, as a brand develops it often becomes necessary for its defining characters to evolve and transform into something new. The role that Steve Jobs played in 1997 when he returned to Apple is a great example of this, for he was intentionally portrayed as the magician, the master of intuition, confidence, action, and creation, who like the Wizard of Oz, used esoteric knowledge to bring about the transformation of the company, and subsequently the transformation of the entire marketplace.

The fact that brands so frequently lapse into irrelevance tells us that there needs to be a more organic, more natural way to manage and develop a brand and to avoid suffering through recurring periods of irrelevance and decline.

One way to think about managing a brand's natural development is in terms of faceting, as we liken this approach to creating a master cut diamond. Many brands have history and dimensionality, various facets that have been carefully developed and which have become familiar in the market. While there is a visible, primary main face to a diamond, secondary and tertiary facets can also be cut to provide additional light and brilliance, shape and symmetry, and thus to contribute depth to the experience of the brand, and create greater value in the marketplace.

A strong and well-developed primary facet of a brand's position thus enables other facets to come into focus and to be leveraged. For example, Nike's original primary facet was running shoes. The company then expanded into other sport footwear categories and later into apparel, then followed by sports equipment.

By gradually developing and displaying additional dimensions, one of the key features of the entire brand experience is its depth, securing for itself the space it needs to grow, change and evolve through new expressions. By strategically considering the sequence by which facets should be developed and shown in particular situations, we augment a brand's core in the most appropriate way, without losing track of its unity. Like light reflected through a brilliantly cut diamond, the business development strategy should devise ways to portray the brand in all its richness.

Apple has developed its brand facets with a compelling product line strategy and its unique naming conventions for an integrated set of products, including the full line of iProducts: iMac, iPod, iPhone, iPad, iTunes, iBook, iCloud, iChat, iCal, iMovie, iWork, iTools, iLife and iPhoto. The "i," of course, was first used in the original iMac itself, launched in May 1998.

By orchestrating integrated value that's intended to make computing on any Apple device more functionally useful with simple and intuitive user interfaces, Apple then extended the brand to achieve the iconic status of a lifestyle brand by enhancing the quality of people's lives and changing their style of communication.

Apple's iPhone 5S ad campaign, *You're More Powerful Than You Think*, shows how the company again applied the personal empowerment theme that has been a part of Apple's brand DNA since the 1990 campaign *The Power To Be Your Best*. By focusing on the human emotional benefits of the iPhone in many different situations, Apple brings brand storytelling to a higher and more soulful level.

Next we'll explore brand positioning in light of some of the soulful branding principles we've been discussing by examining Google. The company has significantly evolved its brand facets since it launched its search engine, and other facets of the Google brand to emerge later comprise a very long list: text search, image search, voice based search, the web browser Chrome, social networking with Google+, Google+ Hangouts, Google+ chat, Orkut, Google Analytics, the operating systems Android and Chrome OS for netbook, its revenue generating services Adwords and Adsense, its email service Gmail, its video file sharing service Youtube, its blogger service Blogger.com, News, Maps, the photo editing and storage service Picata, and Online shopping services, Google Appstore and Google Wallet.

This list exposes a distinctly different approach than Apple, and although Google and Apple are not head-to-head competitors and the products they sell are different, it's worth looking at them side by side. The first thing to note is that while Google is all over the map, Apple has achieved a more organized and unified product architecture, and its brand character as expressed through body, mind and spirit are in far better alignment. This has enabled the fruit company to tap a higher level of hidden brand energy.

Apple has named and claimed its products in a way that reinforces a cohesive brand identity; in terms of defining the character of its brand, Apple is miles ahead. Google is at an earlier stage in its development and is showing early signs of brilliance with its "Parisian Love" campaign, which could be the start of a deep campaign for the brand.

Google is providing invaluable services to society at large, and its "Search On" theme taps into a very important dimension of human life. It's highly profitable with a bright future, but Google has not yet figured out how to leverage and extend the power of a deep campaign to build a more cohesive and powerful character. As a business and a brand, seen in light of the brand planning tools presented here, it falls short of its brand development potential. (A brief discussion of the *Parisian Love* campaign's potential can be found in Appendix 5.)

Another recent development in the "search" market may provide an interesting opportunity to leverage Google's new facets into a new voice. On February 28, 2015 *NewScientist* online magazine reported that "Google wants to rank websites based upon facts, not links." The trustworthiness of a web page might help it rise up Google's rankings if the search giant starts to measure quality by facts, not just links, which would be a major change in Google's search algorithm and present a new characteristic for the brand, yielding more truthful, reliable, and higher quality search results. As the largest gatekeeper of information flow on the World Wide Web, how Google serves up its results will change the nature of our connected, collective consciousness.

And it will change business fortunes as well. Organic search results still account for nearly 70% of search click-throughs, and ad words still account for the lion's share of Google's revenues. If Google follows through with the search algorithm change and you were a brand planner, there would be some significant implications for your brand. Under most search scenarios we all want to know which of the pages served up in the results are the trustworthiest, so if trustworthiness becomes a major characteristic of Google search in the future, instead of counting incoming links, the new system would assess accuracy.

This approach would set up an intriguing brand positioning opportunity for Google, as not only the fastest but also the most factual search engine. In archetypal terms, Google would thereby play the role of ally, guide and mentor, as Obi Wan Kenobi did for Luke Skywalker. Truth is a major leverage point and a highly desirable characteristic for any brand to become aligned with, and with the right execution and planning this could be the foundation of a tremendously effective deep campaign that could further elevate the Google brand.

16 | *The Brand Strength Monitor*

"You can't manage what you can't measure" is an old management adage that is often incorrectly attributed to Dr. Edward Deming. The inspiration behind this old adage comes from Lloyd S. Nelson, director of statistical methods for the Nashua Corporation. Nelson described the difficulty of measuring intangible things in this way: "The most important figures that one needs for management are unknown or unknowable, but successful management must nevertheless take account of them."

In the late 1980s, Nike was the brand of choice for more than 70% of sports oriented teen and college age males. While this indicated brand strength, it also indicated an area of concern. A key question asked, what would happen if the company put together a successful brand campaign to win over women? Would it alienate our competitive male base? This was a question that a new Nike tool called the Brand Strength Monitor, or BSM, was specifically designed to answer, and it became invaluable in guiding the character evolution of that brand.

Nike's approach departed from traditional market-research methods because we weren't tracking the popularity of individual products or individual advertisements, or even advertising campaigns. It wasn't used to pretest creative concepts, and we didn't put any advertising stimulus in the research and ask for feedback on likeability, memorability, or persuasiveness.

Instead, we were looking for a way to gauge the character and personality of the Nike brand, and seeking to understand how target consumer segments felt about the character of the Nike brand. And once we had baseline numbers, it was easy to track variations in the strength of the brand relationship with target groups over time, which became enormously helpful in steering the brand's further evolution and development.

Nike's approach to managing the creative flow of new products was, and is, based on creative exploration and abundance, which means that attempting to pretest concepts and products would have paralyzed the creative force of the company, something Nike's co-founder Phil Knight knew the company had to avoid.

He and the senior marketing team also knew that great brands are built by the quality of the associations and touch points attached to them over time, and that two dimensions could be used to extend the meaning, power and character of the brand.

The first dimension is the physical layer, the products, the distribution system, advertising, the design or look that was unique to Nike, and the efficiency of operations.

The second dimension is the metaphysical layer, which has to do with emotions, how people feel about the brand, the product, and the advertising. The brand guardians knew that the company could do better with more emotionally stimulating brand initiatives. This insight was commonly accepted inside of the management ranks because of the kind of role that sports plays in everyday life. We knew that sports represent a high interest and high involvement category, and many people have strong feelings about participating in and viewing sports.

Nike didn't create most of the feelings people had about sports or fitness, so to access the invisible current of energy that was already flowing through the collective unconscious, Nike just needed to figure out how to tap into it and connect the brand to it in more meaningful ways.

The Brand Strength Monitor was based on a broad survey, a random national probability sample encompassing several thousand interviews per wave. We did three waves per year, and segmented the sample into teen males (13 – 18), teen females (13 – 18), young men (25 – 34), and young women (25 – 34).

We would periodically supplement the sample with other segments, but the core group of early adopters, heavy users, and regular sports shoe buyers were reflected in every wave of the survey.

A big surprise from the first wave of interviews was that more than 70% of teen males named Nike as the brand they desired most. This was a sign of incredible strength but also a sign of vulnerability if we did anything that would alienate this teen and college male base. We also learned from the BSM that fewer than 25% of women had the same feeling. This was a sign of weakness but represented a huge opportunity if we could figure how to appeal to women without changing the male image of the brand.

Nike had a knowledge gap with women, and we needed more information regarding what to do to strengthen the relationship. This admission was a big cultural step for the management team. It led to widening the access point for the brand and 400% sales growth over the next five years.

While the Brand Strength Monitor further confirmed the red flag that Nike had a weakness with women, the depth workshop tool enabled us to expose qualitative insights that generated solutions to fix the problem.

Hence, the Brand Strength Monitor provided Nike with a high level index of brand resonance, like a sonar system whose soundings revealed the hidden contours of the underwater terrain. Brand desirability, values and character descriptions were articulated in considerable detail, through soundings defined as short phrases that described how our target consumers regarded the top three brands in the category.

Sounding feedback told us which brands were wanted most, which were bought last, which consumers would try next, which brands understand the customer best, which offer the most value, which offer the best designs, which are trustworthy and most respected, and which company was one that cared. We also learned about attitudes on an additional broad range of themes, including which was considered to have "heart", which was a good corporate citizen, which was a thought leader, which was arrogant and full of itself, which was empowered people, which was had a sense of humor, which had high ethical standards, and finally which stimulated the most positive feelings.

So while initially the BSM was largely viewed as a novelty inside Nike, for the brand management team it came to be a critically important tool. As you can imagine, this was invaluable information, and when supplemented with sales trends, with media research into share of voice, and other anecdotal evidence such as press clippings and product returns, we had deep and compelling insight into how we were regarded in the marketplace by key segments of people.

For instance, the BSM began to detect a slight softening among teen males in 1993, leading us to discover that the brand was losing its edge and was increasingly viewed as "hype" and lacking substance. When the problem appeared to intensify with the next wave four months later, we immediately fielded depth workshops with alpha teen males, which confirmed these findings, and as a direct result Nike "dialed up the edge meter by signing basketball stars Dennis Rodman and Charles Barkley; Barkley was given the equivalent of an open microphone. 'Role Model' was our working title for a commercial inspired by a passage in Barkley's book *Outrageous!*, in which he complained that parents, teachers, and doctors, rather than athletes, should serve as role

143

models. It was produced two months after these latest somewhat alarming BSM research findings came in."[*]

"Just because I dunk a basketball doesn't mean I should raise your kid," Barkley announced to America, in a commercial that created a record volume of calls and letters to Beaverton that were, interestingly, equally split in favor and opposed. [†]

The BSM later showed that this campaign restored brand image and sales strength with teen males, and it has proven again and again to be an invaluable asset in Nike's brand management toolkit.

Uncovering the hidden drivers of growth and value, ahead of competitors, has always been the Holy Grail of research. Yet, research is frequently most challenged when it comes to defining and tracking "intangibles." The Brand Strength Monitor is an example of an effective way to codify relationship intangibles so they can be measured and monitored for important changes.

This research tool also provides a template for measuring any other kind of intangible value that a corporate management team would want to track. For instance, the tools now exist to build a Corporate Sonar Monitoring system for tracking all the major forms of intangible value. Enterprise-wide intangibles have a lot do with perceptions of adaptability, innovation, intellectual capital, strength of brand, strength of communications, knowledge of consumer needs, skill at leveraging resources, strength of culture, leadership, execution and strategic alliances. Questions that probe facets of each dimension can be designed and tracked. Periodically getting value perceptions from a few key people inside and outside the company on these and other intangible metrics provides perspective on managing expected future value. This is where the real value within a company is being created or challenged.[‡]

---

[*] It's a New Brand World' by Scott Bedbury, Viking Press, 2002

[†] It's a New Brand World' by Scott Bedbury, Viking Press, 2002

[‡] 'Corporate Sonar' designed by Jerome Conlon & Webb Green is an example of an Enterprise Wide Intangible Values Monitoring & Strategic Reporting Tool

17 | *Leadership, Love and Branding*

"The people we are in relationship with are always a mirror, reflecting our own beliefs, and simultaneously we are mirrors, reflecting their beliefs. So relationship is one of the most powerful tools for growth ... if we look honestly at our relationships we can see so much about how we have created them."
— Shakti Gawain

As a discipline, soulful branding occupies a central place between the creative forces and the operational realities in a company. Attaining soulfulness can also require new skills and coordinating mechanisms governing the group of people we call The Brand Guardians, leaders who have responsibility for brand management, marketing, product, advertising, promotion, and communication with C level executives concerned with cultural and future valuation issues.

The Brand Reputation Information Field

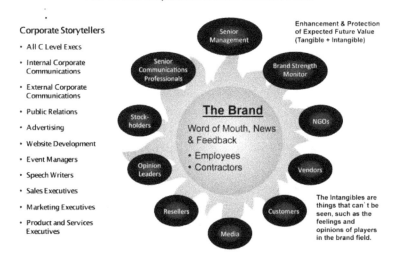

Corporate Storytellers

- All C Level Execs
- Internal Corporate Communications
- External Corporate Communications
- Public Relations
- Advertising
- Website Development
- Event Managers
- Speech Writers
- Sales Executives
- Marketing Executives
- Product and Services Executives

Enhancement & Protection of Expected Future Value (Tangible + Intangible)

Senior Management

Senior Communications Professionals

Brand Strength Monitor

Stock-holders

The Brand
Word of Mouth, News & Feedback
• Employees
• Contractors

NGOs

Opinion Leaders

Vendors

Resellers

Customers

Media

The Intangibles are things that can't be seen, such as the feelings and opinions of players in the brand field.

Most great brand development journeys begin with visionary, soulful leaders who live fully, look clearly into the future, and identify compelling stories about what is possible, and we know from observing great brands that it's entirely possible to improve how a brand is nurtured, developed, protected and projected onto the world.

We also know that if the leaders are not in touch with the soul qualities inside themselves then their companies probably will not advance beyond the simple or traditional business identity forms, and thus will not realize their development potential, which always includes leveraging the power of relationship intangibles. Those vital soul qualities can be expressed in a single word: love.

Love, by which we mean a positive loving regard, a regard for human potential, is an essential quality that must be expressed in abundance by and among the leadership team if an organization is to tap into the hidden energy that exists in potential in the brand field.

Love, as a business idea, may seem out of place for some business leaders, and many consider it out of scope. They pursue less ambitious goals, perhaps defined as increasing profit, or brand awareness, or even developing greater trust.

But love is indeed quite important in business, and it can be a transformative force because the essence of love-driven-leadership is the vision to see each person's talent, potential and dignity developed, as well as the courage, passion and commitment to unlock that potential, and then the loyalty and spirit of mutual support that will energize and unite teams of people working toward shared objectives.

This same approach, high regard and supportive relationships, should also be reflected in the relationships between the business and its customers, expressing the positive role it plays in society and in people's lives, and providing thought leadership to envision still more ideal expressions. Or perhaps instead of "should" we should write "must," for indeed this is a force that is essential to success in the richly complex and dynamically competitive marketplace.

When love-centered leadership takes root on a widespread basis it energizes people and creates unique bonds of team unity to generate a higher level of energy, yielding a powerful "energy advantage" over competing firms that have not tapped this force. Hence, love energy is not just a hidden resource, it's the secret sauce that brings a company and its brands fully to life.

In contrast, if leadership is tyrannical, if employees feel that the culture is driven by fear rather than by a love, then the love energy that could have materialized will never do so, and the results achieved will be diminished. The vital tone of leadership, the voice, character, values and behavior that is modeled by an organization's leaders bring this forth, and doing so is one of their most important responsibilities. And leaders, like everyone else, are shaped largely by their underlying assumptions about how the world works.

Assumptions Lead to Leadership Choices

How each of us sees the world largely determines how we act within it. Eighteenth century philosopher Thomas Hobbes saw humanity engaged in a war with each other over limited resources, resulting in lives that were solitary, poor, brutish and short. This view of the individual as a solitary figure, fearful, alone, and in competition with everyone else still persists, and consequently many business leaders still see society as an uneasy aggregate of self-interested individuals who compete for limited resources, which of course leads to heightened fear, insecurity, greed, hopelessness, and a poverty of spirit.

Consequently, the market economy is largely driven by a self-centered, competitive and hierarchical worldview where what counts most is the accumulation of physical, tangible things. It is by this standard that the global market economy currently is measured through statistics such as GDP, Gross Domestic Production, and PPP, Purchasing Power Parity. These models tell us that the more material goods we produce and consume, the better the economy. Construction of buildings, manufacturing, consumer goods, and transportation, of course, but also weapons, natural disaster relief and rebuilding, post-war reconstruction, and products such as cigarettes are all examples of valued and positive production.

However, the accounts are not in balance, because the environmental pollution that economic activity creates, which diminishes the productive capacity of all natural life support systems, is not currently factored as a cost in the global income accounting system. The negative effects of these non-factored costs are considered simply a cost of lost abundance, but the enduring result is unclean air, unclean water, depleted soils, and high levels of toxicity in our food system. Ironically, the investments required to clean up environmental damage are considered goods, and counted as positive in the global economic reckoning.

Awareness of this imbalance in our accounting methods is increasing. In March 2014, Apple CEO Tim Cook bluntly told an investor who was also a climate change skeptic that he ought to sell his Apple stock holdings if he did not support Apple's initiatives to limit greenhouse gas emissions.* Under Cook's leadership, Apple has pledged to supply 100% of the power it uses from renewable sources. Cook became visibly angry when questioned about the profitability of investing in renewable energy sources.

Cook has also promised to eliminate the use of minerals from the Congo that are sold to fund war and human rights abuses, and these are concerns related to both human ethics, thus love, and to Apple's brand soul. This confrontation may be seen as a character-defining moment for the leadership of the Apple brand, as well as an example of thought leadership showing how corporations can be governed mindfully and soulfully.

While money and investment decisions by themselves do not create meaning in human life, Cook is clearly looking at the broader picture, and he obviously understands its significance to Apple's brand story.

---

*   Tim Cook picks a fight with climate change deniers: Fortune 3/1/14

18 | *The Deep Game*

*"Ideas are like fish. If you want to catch little fish you can stay in the shal-
low water. But if you want to catch big fish, you've got to go deeper. Deep
down the fish are more powerful and more pure. They're huge and abstract.
And they're very beautiful."*
— David Lynch

Soulful branding is a deep positioning game through which brand guardians orchestrate an admirable and holistic brand identity based upon values,
products and stories that really matter.

It starts with that universal essential–a vision.

This is usually how people grasp an idea for the first time, as we make
pictures in our minds to see things that are possible but that have not yet been
created. This is how all entrepreneurs get started. And the vision that starts
any successful business is usually not just a product of the rational mind alone.
Emotions of the founder are usually invested in the idea. And his or her combined thoughts and feelings create a thought/feeling complex that generates
belief and faith in the business model before it is actually performing.

Bringing any model to life requires a sense of physical urgency to get things
done; needed is a sense of strategic urgency to do the right things, the things
that really matter and will be appreciated by prospective customers and inves-
tors.

But beyond the start-up phase, organizational leaders often sense that
something more is possible in positioning their company for greater success.
This feeling is sourced from a need inside exceptional leaders to build something that will last, perhaps even leaving a legacy. For any such leader that has
gotten this far in the book it begs the question: So how do we get started? Is

there a process to embed more soulful and iconic brand principles into how my company operates? This is a great question; the answer is yes, there can be a process developed to take this task on. We will touch on it lightly here. We have executed this process and extensions of it not mentioned here many times inside of successful organizations. This is a process that is proven and works. But we are giving you the very basics here to seed the idea that brand planning is separate from all the other kinds of planning that happens in a company or organization. Brand planning is possibly the highest level of planning, because it's meta-planning–it can touch upon any facet, actual or potential, attached to the business model.

It's important to be clear from the start that this process requires some serious attention and focus by the executive team, because it's a deep game and you're playing for keeps. It takes a long-term view of brand initiatives and their impact and patience and perseverance is required. In most companies, most jobs are concerned with addressing short or mid-term functional or finanical processes and are simply not focused on the long-term positioning of the company. But it's vital... if long-term positioning goals are clearly curated and patiently pursued they can produce a kind of wave coherence that results in a tsunami-sized brand field effect several years down the line.

Business at Hull Speed

In the early stages of establishing a marketing and brand planning discipline at Nike, Jerome used the hull speed sailing metaphor to explain how Nike's business model could be improved, and the recent dramatic enhancement in America's Cup yacht design makes this analogy even more interesting and understandable today.

Imagine if you will, that a corporation is like a sailboat in some important respects. Hull speed is the top speed of a sailboat, which is influenced by the shape of the hull that in turn determines the underwater drag coefficient.

This boating metaphor can inspire brand planners to think about the design of the business model as a means of enhancing the growth rate (speed) of the company. The concept of Hull Speed is relevant to thinking about the design of touch points and brand initiatives. Both the physical and metaphysical layers in your brand determine the hull design of the corporate ship. The kind of sail your brand uses to gather in the spirit of the wind (the brand's social or category zeitgeist) is also a factor in the top speed the corporate ship can attain. The brand communications model in play should work in ways that reduce buyer resistance, social drag or tensions.

In most sailboats the hull speed of the craft is somewhere between 8 to

12 knots. Even with a bigger sail or a motor with more horsepower the boat's speed would not change much, for every degree of increased power to propel the boat faster there is an equal and opposite increase in the underwater drag to match it. So each sailboat has a top speed it can travel under ideal conditions. Hull speed is the top speed in peak power or sailing conditions.

The America's Cup is the world's oldest sporting trophy, with 162 years of sailing tradition. For the August 2013 competition in San Francisco Bay, Larry Ellison, the billionaire CEO and Founder of Oracle, pushed to reinvent the competition into a spectacular television-friendly event, closer to the shore, within view of cheering spectators, concerts and grandstands. But the biggest change was in the sailboat designs that increased wind power and reduced underwater drag.

The new yacht, the AC72 (America's Cup 72 Class), was unlike any that had ever raced in the America's Cup. The 72-foot-long, wing-sailed craft can travel more than twice as fast as the racing sailboats that competed in 2010. When the slick carbon-fiber crafts achieve high speed, both hulls levitate out of the water and begin to fly over the surface on retractable underwater hydrofoils, decreasing drag that can boost the yacht's speed past 45 knots, or 52 miles per hour. It was a surreal sight to see two of these AC72's moving at 50+ mph, close to shore in San Francisco Bay, with gas powered media boats in trail straining to keep up.

Increasing the wing size and ability to trim all wind and underwater contact points tuned the craft for maximum efficiency and speed, and onboard computers helped reduce underwater drag, harnessing still more wind for optimal speed.

The point for us is that many businesses today are operating marketing programs that have a hull speed capable of producing only a small percentage of incremental growth. They use traditional, incremental communication models to inform the market of their presence, and descriptive but prosaic story points to define their public identity, falling far short and failing entirely to overcome social drag by harnessing a more soulful wind.

Higher hull speeds for brands are entirely possible to achieve with more intelligent design, but businesses that focus on meeting only the physical needs of their customers will never harness the latent power of a soulful wind, nor optimize their human growth and development as a company.

Yet some brands have learned to be both efficient and soulful. They have personality and character attributes that project a sense of fun, hipness, intelligence, responsiveness, entertainment, love, compassion, respect for nature and soulful regard in understanding how key relationships are formed.

And while the process of developing and manifesting these soulful branding attributes is a demanding one, as we have seen in all the previous chapters, it's also important to note that having achieved this high level of proficiency, a concerted effort is then required to sustain the results over the long term. For there is always the tendency to revert to the mean, to become average again when the wisdom of the Soulful Brand vision is lost. Another way to express this is to say that entropy, the tendency of things to degrade, is always lurking.

Overcoming Brand Entropy

The word *entropy* refers to a lack of order or predictability, and often signifies a gradual decline into disorder. Brands suffer entropy and decline, more often than not from neglect, and it's essential for brand managers to pay attention constantly and vigilantly to ensure that entropy doesn't occur.

Two astute observers of the history and evolution of civilizations have deep insights to share on the topic of entropy. German historian and philosopher Oswald Spengler believed that each civilization lives by an "idea" that is a concept of its own unique identity, passion, feelings and a sense of its mission and destiny, and that what's important in any civilization (or brand) is the inner passionate struggle to maintain the "idea" against the powers of chaos.*

The "idea" consists of the organizing principles and schemes that marshal the collective energy of people to create an orderly social concept.

British historian and philosopher Arnold Toynbee saw the development of civilization as a series of challenges and responses. Societies (and brands) confront problems and marshal resources, harness energy, and face challenges. To do so requires creative responses, and in Toynbee's view, "the collapse of great civilizations occurs because of a failure of vitality… that is to say an inability to mobilize human energy sufficient to overcome the obstacles" that threaten to undermine the social or brand concept.†

So how does this concept of entropy governing larger social systems apply to the process of monitoring your brand for signs of decay? Below we explore nine topics that brand guardian groups should study to ensure that their brands retain their relevance and vibrancy, and to combat the forces of entropy.

---

* Oswald Spengler: The Decline of the West, 1928, Oxford University Press

† Arnold J. Toynbee: A Study of History, 1946, Oxford University Press

Signs of Brand Entropy

1) Loss of brand difference

Someone inside your company must actively monitor the key brand touch points, both yours and your competitors, to continually track customer engagement. This is a critical job function connected to brand planning; a range of feedback tools and techniques are applicable, from formal and expensive to very informal and inexpensive.

2) Are you using predictable or stale marketing communications?

This is another area where the answer depends upon the relative experience and perspective of the ones asking the question. You may think you're doing fine, on par with all the top brands in your category, but if the entire category is suffering from a tired and stale communications approach, then jumping out of a tired communication model ahead of your competitors is what's required. Be mindful of your core values and the timeless truths while you explore different ways to keep a brilliant campaign concept fresh with creative execution.

For example, both Nike and Pepsi ran deep campaign concepts for more than twenty-five years, freshening them up with new executions every year. During Nike's *Just Do It* years, the company kept its attention focused on its core internal values of Design, Innovation and Inspiration; its core brand values of "authentic athletic performance" never waivered. This perseverance on a big theme and integration with core values can generate a massive coherent waveform that amplifies the voice of the company and helps it achieve a positioning power in the marketplace that is unachievable by lesser means.

Nike's leaders understood the power of this approach at a key turning point in its history in the early 1990s when the economy went soft and its main competitor, Reebok failed with a major campaign "Reebok Lets U B U." Nike correctly anticipated that with softening sales and a softening economy, Reebok would be tapping the brakes on its spending on media. Nike also knew it had a hit with "Just Do It," so the company doubled its media buy, achieving a rapid and pronounced shift in market share, as Nike regained the #1 position in North America, and then the world.

3) Do you understand how communicating well with one segment can narrow your voice in another?

The classic example here is Nike crushing it with competitive males, but missing it entirely with fitness oriented women. The common thread between both market segments, from a core brand values perspective, was the notion of "athletic performance," and when Nike discovered how to interpret "performance" differently for the two groups and yet remain true to its core values in the process, this possibility gave the design and marketing groups latitude to customize the marketing approach to both groups, which led to a massive breakthrough in sales performance for the brand.

4) Are you letting cultural shifts in marketplace or lifestyle behaviors pass you by?

The factors that create social currency are very changeable with the times. Icons, leaders, political ideas, business models, campaigns, themes and urban culture all change along with the issues that people worry about, look up to and talk about. Similarly, the buzz in a culture, the influences in fashion, design, technology, food, beverages, education, entertainment, and all other areas of human interest and the culture industries also change. So periodically weighing in and pondering the ascent and decline of ideas, people, products, brands and social movements is something essential to sustain a brand.

You can learn a great deal by deconstructing why some ideas blow up and become really huge. Why did Michael Jordan reach such iconic heights? There's much more to the answer to this question than just basketball. How is it that Bruce Lee could knock a person across a room with a one-inch punch? There's more going on here than just martial arts mechanics. Why do music genres rise and fall? Who or what is creating strong, indelible imprints on social consciousness? These questions deal with the unfolding social narrative of the times, and for brands that swim in the ether of popular culture, these questions and others like them help to identify new connecting patterns that help keep their brand storytelling fresh.

5) Have you missed competitive shifts that affect your value proposition?

There are two kinds of brands in any category, leaders and followers. A general truth is that it's easier to lead than to follow, and it's more advantageous to lead if your team has tuned instincts and judgments regarding anticipating future consumer needs. But occasionally a competitive threat emerges that requires a response.

In a SWOT analysis (Strengths, Weaknesses, Opportunity and Threats), the first two letters address internal skills, capabilities and assets, while O and T assess external conditions relating to green field opportunity and competitive threats. This exercise gets to the heart of what marketing is as a process by organizing and aligning scarce internal resources and bringing them into sharp focus to achieve an external effect.

6) Are your brand or products growing irrelevant through a lack of change over time?

A provocative statement answers this question: Every product or service category currently falls far short of its development potential! A follower mindset is tracking how you're doing against your competitors on the topic of relevance while a thought leader's mindset extends beyond incremental change initiatives and extends all the way out to, "How can we completely reinvent how people perceive this category and our brand?" This may sound outrageous, but disruptive thinking of this character is actually a smart way of managing the risks associated with changing marketplace dynamics.[*]

7) Is your brand irritating consumers through disruptive communications that rub people the wrong way?

Many companies and ad agencies take pride in the fact that the products and communications they put out into the marketplace produce a polarized response: love it or hate it. And some companies heavy up their media plans so that certain ads burn people out and become irritating, annoying and abrasive. Sometimes highly public messages intended for one group alienate another group. The first step to addressing these issues is to become aware when you're creating them, because there's always a way to fix it once you become aware of it.

8) Is your brand developing an internal management outlook that is insular, arrogant, or complacent?

This can be a really hard question, to which you have to receive really honest answers. This is the realm of hidden values, hidden agendas, protecting old formulas or cash cows, when all the signs are flashing that you've arrived at a strategic inflection point in your brand's journey.

How hard can this be? This type of change management challenge is among the hardest to navigate in business, and the companies that don't navigate such strategic inflection points very well often end up going out of business. So it's a sign of health in your organization's business culture if you can discuss these questions without people getting defensive.

You aspire to reach a higher level, so take a lesson from martial arts: it isn't about beating somebody up; it's about cultivating your soul and spirit. Similarly, branding starts out as a way to beat your competitors, but in the end it's about cultivating the soul and spirit of your own company and its brands.

9) Are you sending out mixed messages or in other ways diffusing your own positioning power?

Sometimes there is a lack of goal congruence between functional units and marketing budgets that are divided up in a way that allows multiple product groups to drive disconnected product positioning initiatives. This is called brand schizophrenia, when a fragmented identity is projected into the market, yielding a much weaker positioning power.

---

[*]   Eating the Big Fish – How Challenger Brands Can Compete Against Brand Leaders' by Adam Morgan is great background reading to sharpen your instincts on this question.

Thoughts, Feelings & Leadership

While brand managers have a critical role to play in overcoming the tendencies toward entropy, and many of the soulful branding tools can surely help them, executives also have a critical role to play in entropy prevention. An excellent way for senior executives to sharpen their brand development concept skills was highlighted in a recent article in the Economist, which examined the benefits that business leaders can get by studying great writers. The article suggested that it's time to replace Outward-Bound leadership courses with Inward-Bound excursions.* They suggest that future leaders should gather at isolated locations during a day, entirely without electronic devices, to concentrate on the studying of a few great books. In the evening, the inward-bounders would then be encouraged to relate what they had read to their own lives and to their business lives. The article went on to argue that a curriculum like this would do wonders for thought leadership.

Indeed, the only way to become a real thought leader is to ignore the noise and go inside one's own consciousness to intuitively and imaginatively find new patterns and paths forward.

Peter Drucker was America's preeminent management guru for 50 years not because he attended more conferences than anyone else, but because he nurtured his mind in great books. He wrote about business alliances, for example, with reference to the marriage alliances found in Jane Austen novels. Reading great works and making abstract connections like this makes the mind more facile and adept at seeing hidden patterns, missed by everyone else. It is the essence of creativity to see connections between things that have never before been connected.

Damon Horowitz, who interrupted his career in technology to get a PhD in philosophy, has two jobs at Google: director of engineering, and in-house philosopher. "The thought leaders in our industry are not the ones who plodded dully, step by step, up the career ladder," he says. They are "the ones who took chances and developed unique perspectives."

Developing Soulful Branding perspective requires sensing new possibilities with all your senses and faculties, not just the management by an objective and hyper-rational mind.

Put a few more arrows in your quiver or a few more lenses in your camera bag.

---

* Economist Magazine: Schumpeter, Philosopher Kings, Business Leaders would benefit from studying great writers. 10/4/14, page 72

Personality Profiles and Branding

According to the typology descriptions in the Myers-Briggs personality profile framework, "Thinking is essentially impersonal. Its goal is objective truth, independent of the personality and wishes of the thinker or anyone else." In contrast, "People (even thinkers) do not like to be viewed impersonally and relegated to the status of 'objects.' Human motives are notably personal. Therefore, in the sympathetic handling of people where personal values are important, feeling is the more effective instrument."

Myers-Briggs indicates that thinking personalities "value logic above sentiment." They "are usually impersonal, being more interested in things than in human relationships... Naturally brief and businesslike, they often seem to lack friendliness and sociability without knowing or intending it." Finally, they "suppress, undervalue, and ignore feeling that is incompatible with the thinking judgments."

In contrast, feeling personalities "value sentiment above logic." They "are usually personal, being more interested in people than in things... Naturally friendly, whether sociable or not, they find it difficult to be brief and businesslike." Finally, they "suppress, undervalue, and ignore thinking that is offensive to the feeling judgments."

From this review of thinking versus feeling types it's obvious that the split between Thinking and Feeling corresponds precisely to the division between objective and subjective. The best market researchers know how to sense for and evaluate these fundamental differences in human perspectives, leading to insights concerning behavior and motivations that can reveal important latent drivers of market behavior.

Breakthrough ideas for bringing your brand to life may come from actions as simple as shifting your mode of perception between thinking and feeling. Sanskrit-based languages have 96 words for love, which allows for a precision of expression far greater than in the West. There is a word for love of your mother, a different one for your father, your horse, the sunset, a poem or your buddy. In India this broad vocabulary for different kinds of relatedness allows people to show affection freely without setting off concerns and fears about what it might mean.

American culture places high value on material things and how much money we can collect. Our thinking and sensation functions have brought the scientific, technological, mechanical aspects of existence to an apex, but we have done this at the expense of our feelings. Huge numbers of people in the

West become lonely, discontented and uneasy, because our capacity for feeling is in a terrible state of disrepair – even worse than India's roads.

This creates an opportunity for a brand planning team, as so many product categories in the West are nearly devoid of meaningful relatedness sourced from feelings. The broader process of brand planning, as described in the following chapter, is intended to provide you with a roadmap to discover, develop, and articulate these powerful, soulful, feeling-oriented qualities and characteristics in your brand.

19 | *Brand Planning as a Process*

> *"A brand is the sum of the good, the bad, the ugly, the off-strategy. Your best product as well as your worst product defines it. It is defined by award winning advertising as well as the god-awful ads that somehow slipped through the cracks, got approved, and, not surprisingly, sank into oblivion. It is defined by the accomplishments of your best employee … as well as the mishaps of the worst hire you ever made. Your receptionist and the music your customers are subjected to when placed on hold also define it. For every grand and finely worded public statement by the CEO, the brand is also defined by derisory consumer comments overheard in the hallway or in a chat room on the Internet. Brands are sponges for content, for images, for fleeting feelings. They become psychological concepts held in the minds of the public, where they may stay forever. As such you can't entirely control a brand. At best you can only guide it and influence it."*
> – Scott Bedbury, A New Brand World

While you don't entirely control your brand, you obviously have tremendous influence over its destiny. You can enlarge its scope, heighten its refinement, develop its critical soulful qualities, and listen carefully in the market as you fine-tune the story elements to achieve optimum resonance with the broader market.

Through this process, while every company is different in culture, size, stage in the broader lifecycle, resources, unique brand DNA and business footprint, there are nevertheless common brand planning phases regardless of your circumstances that you can apply, as we will explore here.

1) The Brand Position Discovery Phase

Appoint a Brand Planner – Brand strategy development requires a champion, someone to put the process in play, deploy research tools, lead meetings, write brand blueprints for growth with integrity linked to the organization's core values, and develop and deploy feedback tools and metrics such as the brand strength monitor. If you are serious about increasing the intangible value of your company through brand development initiatives, you're going to need a brand planner to drive this task, as this is a larger role than presiding over marketing planning, as it works across all business functional groups, even ones not commonly associated with marketing. It requires being able to sense the gestalt of how all activity within the company is affecting perceptions of the company and brand identity. In any medium to large sized company this position is a full-time job, but many companies erroneously add it as an additional responsibility of the CMO or someone in marketing, which can set up a conflict of interest between short-term versus long-term goals.

Identify and Assign Brand Guardians – If you haven't yet created a brand guardian group, this is a very significant step you can take on the road to Soulful Branding. It's a small team, usually 3 – 10 marketing and functional directors who are given strategic responsibilities for enhancing, protecting and preserving brand value. The benefits to the company of a strong brand are so great to the valuation of the company that this reason alone should suffice.*

Usually this group starts with the appointment of a Chief Branding Officer, which for large companies is a full-time position, but it takes coordinated and inspired teamwork to deliver unique, strong, positive and consistent brand experiences to your customers.

Conduct Two Brand Audits – Conduct one focused inside and another on the outside of the company to arrive at an understanding of your current brand position, identify future brand position goals, and assess the gap that exists between what you want people to believe versus what outsiders currently actually know and believe about your brand.

Conduct Brand Gap Analysis – Comparing the difference in perceptions between management's view of the brand and consumers' view is the purpose of a brand gap analysis. This exercise can be a humbling experience if the gap is large, but as we saw in the stories here, at various times both Nike and Starbucks had very wide brand gaps but this didn't discourage their leaders from developing more effective branding strategies and actions. Your knowledge of this gap is of course critical to closing it.

---

* See recommended reading list in the Appendix

2) The Brand Strategy Stage

Brand Guardians Research Review – The brand planner executes and presents the results of brand audits, the internal and the external, to the brand guardians, who then discuss how to build upon strengths and how to remedy the weaknesses.

Conduct a Category Context Analysis – This is the phase in which you scan for "living sound points" and archetypes that may inspire the mythology around your product or brand story. Our great example, Starbucks envisioned the ideal coffee house of the future, and in their analysis the brand planners used their imaginative and creative powers to visualize how the entire category might be reinvented to elevate the consumer experience.

Brand Purpose Review – If you follow the concept of brand ethos or character back to its source you'll arrive at the need to grapple with defining brand purpose and core values. This exercise needs to go deeper than what you might read in a mission statement, as core values defined properly can inspire product design, communications, retail consumer experience and your brand character and differentiation. Thinking deeply about your purpose and values in meeting needs and performing an identity myth is the purpose of this step.

Brand Purpose Gap Analysis – Early improvement opportunities often emerge from this work, and these insights need to be developed and seeded within your organization for immediate benefit and maximum impact.

Figure 4. Brand Stages Map

BrandSpark™ Workshop – A Chief Branding Officer gathers, analyzes and presents to the brand guardians any key facts and findings to date. This review then sets the stage for a Brand Spark Workshop involving all the brand guardians and perhaps additional guests. Concept generation can be formal or informal and include structured mind-burst exercises and stimulus. An offsite meeting or retreat format often works best.

The BrandSpark Workshop initiates the process of aligning strategy and tactics to resolve any brand positioning challenges, and major gaps and positioning issues can be creatively addressed. The brand gap defined in the previous stages provides a perfect set-up for assisting in the design of creative exercises that will enable a group to produce striking brand initiatives. Seed concepts can be sorted and filtered to arrive at the most promising ideas, and once vetted they will become part of your brand initiatives project portfolio that is periodically presented to senior management for a green or red light.

3) The Brand Alignment Stage

A Brand Initiatives Project Portfolio – One end product of a BrandSpark workshop is a portfolio of developed ideas. It usually takes a few weeks of additional work to refine the seed concepts generated in the workshop into full blown possibilities, with finances, rough creative concepts defined and project sponsors identified.

In addition to the brand guardians, senior management, usually including the CEO and other members of the executive team will attend a portfolio review to understand the concepts and remain engaged in brand development. They'll also play the key role of deciding which proposed brand initiatives to execute.

Brand/Marketing Field Alignment – Brand initiatives can be developed independent from marketing campaigns, but it's much better if you find synergies between the two. At this stage the brand planner and marketing directors look for ways to integrate strategies; finding synergies helps develop more coherent waveforms (stories, campaigns, events) that can focus and strengthen your brand positioning activities over time.

4) The Brand Execution Stage

Annual Brand Plan Review – The work in all of the previous stages allows the brand planner to produce an annual Brand Development Plan, which is a roadmap to keep sales, brand image and the internal culture strong for the coming year. Integrated Marketing and Brand Initiatives are executed and launched, often staggered over quarters, to keep the company in the news as the year unfolds, to continue to grow and develop the brand and its positive associations inside and outside the company.

Brand Campaign/Storytelling – Companies with multiple products, product lines, divisions, and far flung geographic territories benefit significantly by not allocating their entire communications budget to product positioning initiatives. Products can be featured in brand campaign ads, but the primary positioning of brand communication is to say something important about the character and values of the company overall and its brand or brands.

The importance of doing brand level communications can't be over emphasized. People use the products but they buy brands. They embrace the unique, strong and positive associations that you can wrap around your products with your brand character. New products will come and go all the time, but brand image is lasting. This principle is sometimes not understood by lower level product line managers and marketing executives whose annual bonuses are tied to the turf they are responsible for, so senior management needs to set guidelines, and set aside some budget for brand level storytelling, as without this you'll fall short of your brand development potential.

Retrospective – An annual review or retrospective of brand positioning status completes the organizational learning loop for the year, and also sets up the planning process for the coming year. The annual review is always a good time to scan laterally across all functions, products and communications for the big emerging ideas that can serve as leverage points in the unfolding of new chapters in your brand story. The retrospective can also be used to scan for meaningful trends in the marketplace and for emerging technologies that your company could employ that would create new value propositions for consumers. Every several years the retrospective should revisit the brand positioning audit process, where personal interviews are performed inside and outside the company to understand the nature of the brand gap.

Brands, Myths, and Stories

If you had a product that you were certain satisfied an unmet need, and you were forming a company and knew nothing about branding, how would you get started? You might call a marketing or advertising agency and ask them for help in discovering and developing your brand concept, and they'd probably suggest starting with the development of a logo, followed by a tagline, and they'd take you through a number of typographic, color and layout options.

Beyond that, they might suggest performing discovery work to understand the heart and soul of your brand, to understand its personality traits and potential positioning themes and language to help you find the brand's public voice. These are tasks related to the subject of your brand ethos and character development, and this work should take into consideration the founder or company values, and how they have been interpreted and expressed in the organization or products.

A very adept brand planner would also look into your brand purpose and how the mission of the brand really intersects and connects with the way people live their lives. This is a very important connecting point for harnessing hidden energy and turning it into intangible value, as the connection between the deeper brand truth and consumer needs then leads into the area of the brand promise, which once discovered, defined and articulated, is the source of the bond that customers have with your brand.

Some brand development work goes further still, and is concerned with the development of a manifesto that presents guidelines for how to speak, human personification characteristics, and tonal communication guidelines. All brands must know who their target audience really is, not as numbers on a spreadsheet but as living, breathing human beings. This kind of in-depth consumer profiling sometimes goes by the world of psychographics, but it's possible to go beyond psychographics if you conduct depth workshops.

It can also be helpful for brand guardians to establish guidelines for new initiatives to make sure that new products, services, or marketing projects fit within the framework of the brand concept. Some also develop brand fit screening criteria to help in evaluating new products, projects or initiatives for alignment with the brand concept.

The iconic brands we used as examples here generally fall into this category, and while advertising agencies can help smaller companies accelerate their brand development process, most of the largest Soulful Brands experience an organic internal growth process where the brand meaning and purpose, its values and voice evolved over years and even decades inside the culture of the company.

Some of these Soulful Brands got to a stage, as Nike did in 1986, of appointing internal guides and brand guardians to help with the branding process, planning frameworks, the crafting of brand research tools, brand problem solving and strategic planning. Reflecting the power of this work, from 1986 to 1996 Nike brand sales grew by 814 percent, nearly doubling each year under the guidance of a very attentive team of brand managers and senior level guardians.

The kinds of brand discovery and development problems that Nike faced during that ten-year period were new and uncharted. There weren't any brand development guidebooks at the time, and the problems themselves were largely undefined and ill structured. As lead scouts and guides, we often had to enter the forest where there was no path and create a path, and in the process we created many unusual and unorthodox ways of viewing problem solving, product needs finding, customer relationship development, cultural bridge-building, and how to think about breakthrough communications.

So while branding is a very old art form, one practiced by kings, wise men, potters, livestock owners, creators of myths, national leaders, tribal chieftains, magicians, scientists and business people, there is still great opportunity to discover and create new methods and tools, to extend the art.

Jan Assman notes that humans are often just like spiders, as we weave invisible threads and patterns of experience that create the sticky meaning in our lives.* When you look at Egyptian architecture and hieroglyphs, at the statues and the burial chambers, the hidden web of meaning, what they believed in, what they valued, and what they worshipped is all exposed. Brand research today can resemble the process of performing an archeological dig of an old world civilization, yet instead of digging through layers of history in the dirt, we're digging through layers of meaning in the mind and in the heart and soul.

In the legend of the building of Solomon's Temple we find an example of cultural and religious meaning embedded in a sacred text. The temple was built in accord with sacred geometry, and the significance of this building and its symbolic meaning has been passed down through the millennia, influencing the hidden rights and rituals of the Masons, and also helping to shape architectural patterns in key buildings in Washington D.C.

Human beings are storytellers. We like stories, so when you offer to tell a young child a story she will clasp her hands in anticipation of the joy it will bring. She expects pleasure, and hopes for an experience that will excite her imagination and transport her to emotional places she will enjoy visiting. And this love of a good story stays with us throughout our lives.

The myths that groups of people create are the stories that define a society's values and beliefs, and those myths can long outlast the people who first tell them. The beautiful myths of Greece, kept alive within Greece in the theatre, influenced the destiny of the people who created them. When they were still fresh, belief and pride in them were enough to bring scattered tribes into

---

* The Mind of Egypt – History and Meaning in the Time of the Pharaohs' by Jan Assman, Metropolitan Books, 1996

confederations, and then they gave inspiration to sculptors and poets of an art and literature that remain unsurpassed in human cultural history.

And long after the glory that was Greece had faded, they have passed over to the literatures of the modern world and given to all peoples, including the Greeks, a poetic expression of the nobility and possibility of the human soul.

All myths are creative products of the human psyche, creative manifestations of humankind's universal need to explain psychological, social, cosmological and soulful realities, and those who tell them are a culture's mythmakers and brand builders.

Stories and myths help people to better see, feel and understand what is important. Yet advertising and entertainment media today are saturated with shallow messages and relatively few meaningful stories. This is a void that creates huge opportunities for companies operating in high interest and high involvement categories where short form and branded content storytelling in videos and apps is possible. When you develop and refine your art of storytelling and reward your audience with meaningful and entertaining stories, you can simultaneously stand out, say something important, and strike emotional chords. This is the communications sweet spot responsible for building great brands.

Myth making, storytelling and brand building journey over common ground when a company's brand leadership learns to think on new levels about possible business narratives. What gives your brand and company life is how your brand is regarded by the people you touch, not by how many people can identify your logo.

Yet there are many different kinds of brands. Some have small budgets and a simple identity, while others have a more rich and layered set of associations that accumulate over a long period of time. Some of the more complex brands have developed more soulful and iconic identities, but you don't need a huge amount of resources to become soulful and iconic. What GoPro has done with video storytelling, much of it consumer sourced, and what FullSail University has achieved by embedding on their website a higher level of the digital design, entertainment and media arts tools, are two examples of a modest budget, finely tuned, reaping enormous brand development rewards.

And while visionary founders get the brand journey started, neither the founders nor the executives ever fully own a brand. Instead, brands live inside of human experience, and the most you can do is influence and guide what you'd like people to experience, but you cannot experience it for them, nor force them to experience it as you wish them to.

20 | *The End Game: Aligning Commerce and Culture*

"Who you are is speaking so loudly that I can't hear what you're saying."
– Ralph Waldo Emerson

"The most important thing in communication is hearing what isn't said."
– Peter Drucker

This chart shows exactly why branding has become so important.

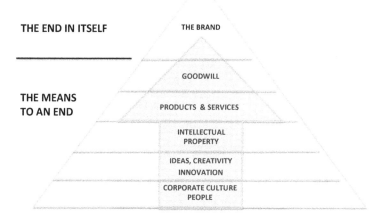

Figure 5. The Brand as Process Pyramid

While brand planners are concerned with all levels of this brand pyramid, clearly it's at the top that the payoff comes. For ultimately it's the brand that becomes the enduring story as well as the compelling asset for the future of the organization.

The Brand Development Pyramid

The final result of putting Soulful Branding principles into play is to create a more healthy and sustainable organization.

On the strictly business side of this equation, increasing a brand's attractiveness to widening circles of consumers supports market share and sales growth, premium pricing, customer and employee loyalty, and enables brand extensions to broaden the addressable market. But there is another side to consider as well. There's the internal culture of the company to consider. Anything that strengthens that culture, meaning strengthening the quality of the relationship that people have with the company, this taps into hidden field energies and resonance that can make all the difference and give your company an intangible energy advantage.

The Brand Development Pyramid shown below describes a series of attributes from bottom to top that encompass the two common levels of branding: the basic or rational level concerned with a sharp focus on positioning the products you sell around the functional benefits they deliver, and the meta-rational level of branding, which is where brand guardians are concerned with giving products identities that resonate deeply with human values, specifically embedding a product with heart and soul values that emanate from a brand's DNA. The tools for conducting the meta-rational level branding are the very same tools that we've identified in Soulful Branding. This brand pyramid was initially developed to support brand level communications as opposed to product level positioning.

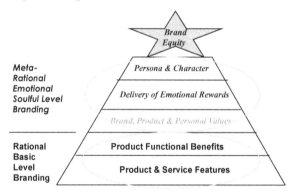

Figure 6. Meta-Rational Branding Pyramid

What we've discovered in our branding journey is that given a choice, people generally choose brands with more admirable character traits.

The Human Development Pyramid

"The story of the human race is the story of men and women selling themselves short."

— Abraham Maslow

Abraham Maslow described the progress toward a person's full development as a hierarchy of needs in his very well known, 1943 paper, "A Theory of Human Motivation."* This model has been widely accepted, adapted, and built upon, as it expresses some key truths about the individual's aspirations and the stages that each one goes through on the journey of self development.

Figure 7. *Maslow's Hierarchy of Needs*

This pyramid shows basic human needs at the bottom beginning with the physical, and then needs related to safety and security, which encompasses factors such as employment, and access to basic resources, family, health and property security. Love and belonging needs come next and include friendship, family and intimacy. Esteem needs including confidence, achievement, respect for others and respect by others are on the fourth layer.

These four levels are considered "deficit needs" because until they are satisfied, movement to the highest realm is thwarted. Once they are met, at least to some degree, then the individual can move to higher levels of psychological development related to self-actualization. At this level a person strives to become more autonomous, self-directed, creative, spontaneous, lacking prejudice and working on transcendent goals.

The point for us, of course, is that Maslow's pyramid very closely mirrors the process of organizational and brand development for many companies. Amazingly, however, in many categories the competing brands are fighting positioning battles at the two lower rungs of this ladder, seemingly unaware of the much greater potential that lies in the upper tiers.

Many companies start out by articulating a 'bare bones' business model and a functional brand concept, with very little attention to identifying or articulating more abstract positioning, underlying values or deeper character. Most beginning brands are basic brands that are built around a simple graphic identity, focusing on the physical or other deficit needs only.

---

* Abraham Maslow: A Theory of Human Motivation (1943)

In contrast, brands with soul have an emotional underpinning and our work as described here has shown definitively that the higher up the brand guardians aspire to go, the more opportunity there is for uniquely positioning a brand and evoking admirable character traits.

Brand soul is sourced from core values of your company. It doesn't come from a product positioning statement. As *Just Do It* expressed the deeper soul of Nike and *Think Different* described the soul of Apple, the pursuit of higher-level themes projects an energetic spirit that makes a brand lively, human, and accessible. What expresses the deeper soul of *your* company?

The pursuit of a soulful brand, then is not only an expression of individual, group, and organizational commitment, it's also an expression of shared intent, and likewise it's a means of establishing very high goals that are worth striving for, not only for the good of a brand and a company, but for the greater good of society. Soulful branding can't therefore be subverted by more mundane commercial objectives, but rather raises the significance of commerce to a higher level of development of a people, a community, and a culture.

Soulful branding thus brings commerce and culture into harmony in a way that proposes to move the marketplace forward by addressing the deeper, more fundamental human needs and aspirations, those which also bring out the best in us individually and collectively. In this way we discover that doing the best for the brand itself, creating commercial success, does not come about in spite of our humanity, but rather in service to it. This is the greatest aspiration that commerce can aspire to, and the pursuit of soulful branding can therefore contribute significantly to this highest of goals.

21 | *The Soulful Story Behind 'Amazing Grace'*

We close with the story of John Newton, a sea captain who was involved in a remarkable incident in the year 1748.

His ship was made of wood and powered by huge square rigged sails, all hand crafted, so each ship was a work of art powered by the gifts of the wind. On this particular journey Captain Newton sailed from London, heading south down the coastlines of the Old World to pick up his cargo, and then turned to sail to the New World across the ocean. About half way across the Atlantic he noticed the swells starting to increase, causing the ship to rock and sway unusually. He sensed trouble ahead.

The swells started getting bigger, the ocean became choppy, and the wind picked up. Captain Newton realized that perhaps he was a little late in the season for an Atlantic crossing, and that there could be a major storm ahead. Conditions continued to get worse, and worse, and worse.

The ship's wheel, the steering column, had to be held at all times, because if you let go the rudder would turn completely, causing a ship to spin one way or the other. A man was needed on deck to stand at the ship's wheel at all times, no matter the weather or situation; that man was usually the captain. And so this is where Captain John Newton found himself that day, on the deck as the storm began to set in, holding onto the wheel of his ship.

As conditions continued to worsen, he had his men climb up the ship's tall masts and pull down all the sails.

In such a storm, as the waves started to increase in height and occasionally spilled over the top of the ship, it was common for crew members to tie themselves to parts of the ship because if the ship were to break apart in the storm at least each man would have something to hold onto.

And what, oh what was being transported as cargo on John Newton's ship? Below the decks one would not find wine, olive oil nor textiles. Below the deck were over one hundred people chained to the floor, for Newton was in the business of transporting slaves.

They could hardly move, and now they were subject to the rising swells and resulting seasickness, which soon turned into ten foot and occasional twenty-foot waves crashing over the sides of the ship and spilling huge quantities of icy-cold seawater on top of them.

After they pulled all the sails down Captain Newton sent his men below. Large quantities of water were by then spilling into the ship, and Newton feared absolute and final calamity. It was all he could do to hold onto the ship's wheel, and so he chained his second-in-command to the wheel; if the ship began spinning it would be doomed by the onslaught of the swells.

The storm became torrential, and it rained so hard that Newton could barely even see what was in front of him, let alone direct the ship perpendicular into the swells to avoid a deadly, parallel slap by giant waves that would have quickly bust the ship's frame apart.

Meanwhile, the slaves down below, who could see nothing of what was going on, jarred and jerked on the ocean with torrents of ice-cold salt water pouring over them every few minutes. Instead of screaming, crying, yelling, wailing, and demanding, they began to sing a prayer that came from the Ah-Om languages that originated in ancient Egypt. The song had no lyrics, just tones, and they sang so loudly that Captain Newton heard the ancient hymn even over the roaring sound of the wind and rain in what was rapidly deteriorating into hurricane conditions.

Over and over they delivered it like a mantra, an affirmation, while the conditions on that deck became so intense that Newton, as he stood lashed to the wheel of the ship, began to sing too. Just to keep his sanity he began to make up lyrics, fitting them to the song he heard coming from the enslaved people below.

At the climax of that dreadful evening, when the rain was torrential and he was so exhausted that he could barely stand or hold onto the wheel, he was only able to continue at his post because of the power of the voices coming from the people down below. They continued to sing in spite of their captivity, their distance from home, and being on the brink of death.

And at that moment Captain Newton swore that if he made it – if they all made it – he would let them all go, surrender his shipping license, and become a minister.

Captain John Newton made it through that dark night, and everyone aboard survived the death defying experience. The storm passed, the sails were put back up, and they turned the ship around and set sail back to Africa to return the slaves to their homes. Newton then sailed back to London, turned in his shipping license, became a minister, and wrote down the lyrics of the still-present and well-tuned song that guided him through that stormy night.

The song is called Amazing Grace, an ancient African prayer accompanied by English lyrics.

Captain John Newton's story flows down through the ages due to its power to touch us deeply, to reach to the very core of our humanness. His story touches the archetypal soul powers of inspiration based on courage, will, song, compassion, and joining together as one human family. It continues to inform us that no matter what situation we face, when there is a way out there is a great power that can be invoked as an expression of Grace.

Through the influence of the heart, channeled in communication through song, we are able to direct our soul power to the ship's captain although totally unconscious of his own crimes, giving the strength to make it through the night, transform our being, turn the ship around, and save rather than destroy lives.

The captive slaves could well have responded with many emotions – rage, despair or terror among them, but what they chose instead was love, beauty, and dignity in the form of a song-prayer directly from the soul, a song-prayer so monumental that it saved them all, and still touches us today.

Your brand may not have the power to transform a man from a slave trader into a minister, but it is well within your grasp to express through your brand the very highest and best of the human soul qualities, to express deep character conviction and to channel human aspiration toward all the things that are good, true, and beautiful. This quest is the union of commerce and culture, and it is in service to the best that we can be and become that a truly soulful brand finds its way.

Appendices

A | *Key Concepts*

A Brand's Interactive Field … is the hidden perceptions and feelings people have when they interact with any of your products, communications or brand. Sales and market share trends suggest issues and opportunities in your brand field. Dreams, archetypes, and ideal states are also dormant forms of energy in the brand field.

Brand Strength or Weakness … is your relative standing compared to other brands in the category, determined by qualitative or quantitative research methods.

Brand Position Analysis … is a strategic research technique used to understand how your brand identity, persona and character are defined both inside and outside of the organization.

Brand Gap … is the difference between how the leaders inside your company want your brand to be perceived and how consumers and prospects outside your organization actually perceive it.

Category Context Analysis … is the use of archeological and psychological research techniques to map the cultural and consumer mind-space surrounding a product, archetype, or collective marketplace behaviors within a category, with the aim of identifying the drivers, unmet needs and category development potential.

Brand Drivers … are the key brand strategies and tactics that simultaneously generate sales, enhance image and strengthen the internal culture. Sometimes business goals are defined too narrowly using only financial metrics, so the concept of brand drivers conveys the principle that some sources of growth have greater power to also strengthen the brand concept and brand field energy in play.

The Big Dig … is a comprehensive strategic brand position and potential study and plan that uses multi-visioning techniques to expose brand gaps and category development potential. Jerome Conlon and Scott Bedbury at Starbucks pioneered this technique in the mid 1990s.

Early Brand Planning Considerations … means starting by considering the health of the business and clearly defining what's going well, what's not, and which are the areas where performance is a concern. Identify the top 4 to 5 concerns that relate to the quality of contact in developing the consumer or market segment relationships.

Research Analysis Linked To Brand Strategy … addresses the question, What do the latest consumer research findings tell you about market dynamics, your brand strength, and customer satisfaction in your category? The marketplace is rapidly changing, especially with new marketing and research technologies, so it's important to track your brand's strength in trend data to be able to see it rising or falling.

Research Synthesis … because research must always be interpreted, from data-to- information-to-insights-to-inspiration. In any given review period, the top 4 – 5 brand issues should be sorted, and initiatives developed to address them. Taking brand identity lightly or for granted is a sure route to becoming irrelevant.

Unique Brand Differentiator … reflects the principle that key insights into brand differentiation should be connected to a company's core passions, and to what people outside the company really care about.

Branding Strategy … is based on marketing plans that provide the basis for the brand strategy blueprint. Marketing plans tend to be focused on achieving product and sales goals, while stronger brand character can also help achieve these goals in a less direct fashion. Generating brand initiatives, which are projects that strengthen the brand-to-customer relationship over time within key products, lines, or market segments, sources brand Strategy.

Strategic Brand Plan … is a document that can also go by the name of a Brand Roadmap or a Brand Blueprint for Growth. Periodically a brand concept generation workshop can be executed by internal brand guardians and outside experts who can add new creative perspectives. The result of the workshop can be a portfolio of brand initiative ideas that have been screened, vetted and financially approved. This list of brand projects and the context of why they are needed, what the company hopes to attain, and how results will be measured is called a Strategic Brand Plan. This plan generally looks into the future two or more years.

Branding Tactics … result from the process of implementing annual brand plans and monitoring all projects for completion, quality and positioning impact. This includes feedback systems such as a brand strength monitor to provide feedback on brand positioning or key campaign or project performance.

The Current State ... is assessed at least once a year, when leaders do a detailed analysis of performance to evaluate what went right and wrong. A brand 'State of the Union' report identifies the key challenges the brand faces and defines a roadmap of initiatives looking several years out.

The Ideal State ... envisions the brand as it ought to be positioned, how you want the majority of people to think, feel and associate with your brand, and what you want them to believe, value and remember. The ideal future state makes it possible to put plans in place year after year to achieve this ideal.

Brand Truth ... is also called Brand DNA; see below.

Brand DNA ... is the central truth behind the brand purpose. Sometimes it's defined by a brand mantra, a three-word centering phrase like Nike's "Authentic Athletic Performance," and sometimes it's defined in a graphic representation of concepts, like in the blueprint of a building with levels for different floors.

Brand Purpose ... is a one-sentence phrase, usually arrived at through introspection, about a brand's reason for being. Nike's purpose, for example, is "To bring innovation and inspiration to the athlete in all of us."

Core Values ... is, for example, a list of the key attributes or subject areas in which your brand will strive mightily to differentiate and distinguish itself. For Nike it's "Innovation, Inspiration, Design and Authentic Athletic Performance," and with women the company learned a new one called, "empowerment." At Starbucks it's "specialty coffees, the perfect roast, the perfect cup, uplifting coffeehouse experiences."

Brand Bible ... is the brand logo, graphic arts and visual design language standards manual.

Brand Intangibles ... are, for example, innovation, thought leadership, adaptability, design, human relationship strengths, communications prowess, salience, relevance, resonance, internal culture, values, admirable character traits and focus.

Brand Mojo ... is the positive feelings and attraction (like sexual attraction) that a brand generates from a virtuous orchestration of its intangibles.

Brand Qi ... builds on the Oriental word for "life force," which refers to the hidden force inside the human body that animates it. Brands also possess "Qi," which is embodied in an internal group of visionaries and guardians. The spirit, energy and vision within the brand guardian groups generate Brand Qi.

Goodwill ... reflects how your brand reputation, intangible value and intellectual capital are expressed on your company's balance sheet, and when the company is sold reflects the value paid above the book value of the net assets.

Brand Equity ... is the commercial value that derives from consumer perception of the brand name of a particular product or service, rather than from the product or service itself.

B | *18 Questions for Brand Guardians to Consider*

These 18 questions will help you kick-start discussions about intangible value creation so that you can begin harnessing the power of the energy hidden in your brand field. They are presented in two separate lists, one dealing with harnessing the power of brand intangibles, and a second on failure modes to avoid.

On harnessing the power of Brand Intangibles:

1) Are you transcending a product only relationship with your customers?
Your brand ethos or character can be communicating something to your public beyond the functional benefits of your products. Yet many marketing plans are hyper focused on driving product benefits home in marketing communications, and there is no budget left to say anything important about the brand. If this is happening inside your company then you should regard this as a misallocation of resources, and an example of a misalignment between short-term marketing goals and long-term brand positioning goals.

2) Are you connecting your brand to powerful and timeless emotions?
Stories and communications that simultaneously engage body, mind and spirit are far more powerful than rational arguments or bullet point checklists. Human life has far more dimensions than that, so spend some time thinking about how to make your communications briefs more inspirational. Expand your worldview on storytelling. Read a book on screenwriting.

3) Will your product innovation initiatives be meaningful in the marketplace?
The first assessment of this question will be a gut check by executives with financial approval authority. You can increase the confidence by fielding a cross-functional team to do a circuit test of meaningfulness related to leadership's own intuition and feelings. When products prototypes are ready, and if a large rollout investment is required, then you can conduct a simulated product

trial and user satisfaction study to pre-assess its likely success. In some companies like Nike, with thousands of new products launched each year, other more efficient methods for assessing new product ideas can be created, such as Nike's future's program (described above).

4) Are you innovating in your marketing communications and achieving resonance?
Resonance is one of three principles in evaluating whether or not a piece of communication is really breaking through; the other two are salience and relevance. Hit advertising campaigns, depth campaigns that become viral social memes in a culture, don't happen every day. Creating them is a worthwhile objective, though, and sometimes a viral video can be produced for extremely low cost. But it's far more likely that you'll achieve solid results if you have an agency or branded content studio lead the work.

5) Have you become a cultural or a category protagonist for the consumer experience?
Answering this question is the whole point of conducting a category context analysis. In this analysis you scan the entire category for energy levels, vitality and issues. If you were to perform this kind of analysis for the fast food category what would you find? Many of the Quick Service Restaurant formats are distant imitations of McDonalds, using bright, clown-like colors, vinyl composite tile, glass and chrome surfaces, bluish fluorescent internal lighting, counters, bright menu boards and the smell somewhere from the back of a deep fryer. A visual brand audit and a touch points audit would present in a single presentation all the repeating themes, colors, textures, styles in use so that you can take it all in at a glance and ask questions such as, Where is the differentiation? Who has a unique character and value proposition? Then you're set to ask the next question: If we had a blank slate, what could the QSR business become? If we wanted to be the protagonist for the QSR Category, to redefine it in a more ideal state, when it's as good as it gets, then what would we change?

6) Have you updated and refreshed your marketing model lately?
Markets and competing marketing activities can change the brand landscape very quickly. If you're not making periodic investments to freshen up your approach to marketing then your brand will be left behind and begin to suffer from decreasing freshness and relevance. The marketing models for many companies today have embraced digital marketing looking for synergies where possible with bricks and mortar. Digital can dramatically lower the cost of finding your audience and making them aware of something new, and social

media tools are showing great promise for well-crafted products and campaigns.

7) Could it be worthwhile to better tailor our products or services to individual segment needs?
To answer this question requires a segmentation study that is designed around finding out which benefits are sought most by different groups of people (men vs. women; heavy users vs. light users; young vs. older, etc.). A segmentation study will also allow you to get a better profile of segments, and quantify the size of the market opportunity to let you know if any particular segment is really worth pursuing.

8) Are you using brand architecture and design wisely, to broadly appeal to different kinds of tastes?
This is a gut check question that requires that the person or group evaluating the question has design sensibility or vision. If you're company doesn't have a strong design sensibility then you are missing out on one of the major leverage points in the positioning game. There are architectural firms, retail store design firms, product designers, ad agencies and even brand architecture firms that can show you what a stronger design perspective could accomplish for your brand. Many companies choose to bring critical design skills in-house because within the global competitive marketplace, design itself has emerged on one of the main brand leverage points.

9) Have you located your brand purpose and core values?
To assess this question you may find yourself in murky waters. As in the Nike blind spots story above, the cultural waters that executives and employees are all swimming in are invisible, as this story explains. The little fish went to the queen fish and said, "I have always heard about the sea, but what is this sea? Where is it?" The queen fish explained, "You live, move and have your being in the sea. The sea is within you and without you, and you are made of the sea, and you will end in this sea. The sea surrounds you as your own being."
This story points to the challenges of both executive assimilation and brand planning, the challenges that relate to tacit beliefs that govern the worldview of the company, its leaders, and how things get done. Sometimes these hidden beliefs are called sacred cows, and they can be "limiting beliefs," as Nike discovered in its false assumptions about women's needs, which weren't well formed, and which tacitly followed a macho male sports model.
This system influences all the other touch points and determines how engaging the brand really is, so the process of diving deeper into your brand purpose

requires you to step back and gain perspective. It may require doing a little research or homework; it may require asking new questions and getting a few people together whose opinions really matter, and asking them about core values and perhaps the need to develop a greater understanding of the value system inside the company.

Major failure modes to avoid in branding

10) Loss of your brand difference
Unless someone inside your company is actively monitoring and tracking key touch points, both yours and competitors, then you're vulnerable here. Addressing this is one of the job functions connected to brand planning, and a budget for brand strength monitoring is required. There is a range of feedback tools and techniques – from informal and inexpensive, to very formal and expensive – depending upon the nature, scope and needs of your organization.

11) Are you using predictable or stale marketing communications?
This is another area where the answer depends upon the relative experience and perspective of those asking the question. You may think you're doing fine, on par with all the top brands in your category, but the entire category may be suffering from a tired and stale communications approach.
Jumping out of a tired communication model ahead of your competitors is what's required, but one caveat here involves being mindful of your core values and timeless truths versus the need creative change on the surface. It's always better to be anchored in your values and brand truth from which you can explore different ways to keep a brilliant campaign concept fresh with new creative executions. For example, Nike ran the Just Do It campaign over twenty-five years, freshening it up with new angles in new eras. During this period Nike's attention to its core values of Design, Innovation & Inspiration and to its internal brand mantra "authentic athletic performance" never waivered. This perseverance on a theme and integration with core values generates a massive coherent waveform that amplifies the voice of the company and helps it achieve its positioning goals.

12) Do you understand how communicating well with one segment can narrow it within another?
The classic example here is Nike really crushing it with competitive sport males but missing it entirely with fitness-oriented women. The common thread between both market segments from a core brand values perspective was the

notion of "athletic performance," but how men driven by sports defined performance compared with how women driven by fitness defined it were two totally different things. When Nike learned it could interpret "performance" differently for the two groups and still stay true to its core values in the process, it gave the design and marketing groups permission to customize the marketing approach to both groups, which led to a massive breakthrough in sales performance for the brand.

13) Are you letting cultural shifts in marketplace or lifestyle behaviors pass you by?
What creates social currency is very changeable with the times. Icons, leaders, political ideas, business models, campaigns themes and urban culture all change with the times. What people worry about, look up to and talk about ... the buzz in culture, the influence in fashion, design, technology, food, beverages, education, entertainment, and all other areas of human interest and the culture industries change. Periodically weighing in and pondering the ascent and decline of ideas, people, products, brands and social movements can greatly benefit a major brand.

You can also learn a lot by deconstructing why some ideas become huge. Why did Michael Jordan reach such iconic heights? There was much more going than just basketball. How was it that Bruce Lee could knock a person across a room with a one-inch punch? There was more than just martial arts mechanics. Why do music genres rise and fall? Who or what is creating strong, indelible imprints on social consciousness? These are the questions that deal with the unfolding social narrative of the times, and for brands that swim in the ether of popular culture these questions can help identify new connecting patterns to keep their brand storytelling fresh.

14) Have you missed competitive shifts that affect your value proposition?
A SWOT analysis – Strengths, Weaknesses, Opportunities and Threats – can help to identify and address significant threats. The first two letters, S and W, assess internal skills, capabilities and assets, while the second two assess external conditions relating to green field opportunity or competitive threats. This exercise gets to the heart of what marketing is as a process by organizing and aligning scarce internal resources and bringing them into sharp focus to achieve an external effect.

15) Is your brand or products growing irrelevant through a lack of change over time?
A provocative statement related to this question is this one: "Every product or service category currently falls far short of its development potential." A

follower mindset is tracking how you're doing against your competitors on the topic of relevance, while a leader's mindset extends beyond incremental change initiatives all the way to, "How can we completely reinvent how people perceive this category and our brand?" Disruptive thinking on this level is a smart way to manage the risk associated with changing marketplace dynamics.

16) Is your brand becoming irritating to consumers through disruptive communications that rub people the wrong way?

Many companies and ad agencies take pride in the fact that the products and communications they put out into the marketplace produce a polarized response, love it or hate it. And some companies heavy up their media plans so that specific ads burn people out and become irritating, annoying and abrasive. Further, some highly public messages intended for one group may alienate another group. These are challenges that needed to be guarded against, and which thoughtful planning and briefs can be overcome. The first step in addressing this issue … is to become aware that you are creating this issue. There's always a way to fix it once you recognize it.

17) Is your brand developing an internal management outlook that is insular, arrogant, or complacent?

This can be a hard question to ask, but one to which you must receive really honest answers. Here we're in the realm of hidden values, hidden agendas, protecting old formulas or cash cows, and when all the signs are flashing that you've arrived at a strategic inflection point in your brand's journey you must act. How hard is this to do? This kind of change management challenge is among the hardest to navigate, and many companies don't navigate strategic inflection points at all, and end up going out of business. The average life span of a corporation is only 40 years, and this is one of the major reasons why.

18) Are you sending out mixed messages or in other ways diffusing your positioning power?

Are you creating your own tower of Babel? Sometimes companies lack functional goal congruence, and when the marketing budget gets divided up in a way that allows multiple product groups to drive disconnected product positioning initiatives the result can be brand schizophrenia, where a fragmented identity with a much weaker positioning power is being projected.

C | *Chief Brand Officer*

Questions, Concerns & Responsibilities

Branding and marketing are both processes of generating, managing and controlling ideas and resources to focus them on serving people in some way outside of the organization and reaping rewards. The Chief Branding Officer's role in the leadership of the brand guardians group is to cultivate what is heroic and great about a company, its brand, its products and services, and the internal organizational culture. All of these ingredients are inter-related and work synergistically to develop strong brands.

Chief Brand Officers scan operations and the outside world in the search for opportunities, knowing that adaptation is the key to survival in any business eco-system. The brand is like a person, as it is a living, breathing open energy system with many human characteristics. The CBO knows that there is often a gap between what people on the inside believe about the brand compared with what people on the outside believe, and that to close this gap requires a special focus on core values and how they are expressed in the operations of the business and in marketing.

CBOs know that striving for too much control and consistency can create a two dimensional, cardboard character of a brand image. To battle this they strive to make their brands multi-dimensional in a cultural sense, and often a protagonist for some worthy cause. CBOs also know that being a brand protagonist means creatively embracing the use of tools including art, design, innovative thinking, ideation workshops, digital technology, storytelling, and finding ways to place your product or service inside of a broader context that solves problems and somehow elevates the human spirit.

What else should Chief Branding Officers be concerned with? In our experience here are six key questions.

1. How can we build & nurture a better brand?

One person in your organization needs to be tasked with thinking about the question as an ongoing inquiry, and creating conversations and forums where this question is examined repeatedly through the year.

2. How can we achieve a sustainable advantage?

In recent years, art, design, branded content storytelling with higher entertainment values, character merchandising, technology innovation, Apps, social media, viral videos, and online community development and other themes have allowed brands to develop resonance in new ways. It is the CBO's task to constantly explore to identify new developments and possibilities.

3. How can we develop internal brand stewards?

Tapping people to participate in the brand guardians group is the easiest way to do this, but the group gatherings and processes needs to be led effectively to achieve meaningful results. There are also internal speeches, videos, rallies that the CBO can be involved with that lifts the internal culture.

4. How can we achieve integrated marketing synergies?

The easiest way to do this is to create coordinating mechanisms in the form of review meetings where people leading the development of marketing and brand campaigns get together to examine those campaigns, assess their results, and discuss potential synergies.

5. As we strive for creativity and diversity in our work, how can we avoid chaos, lack of focus, and energy dissipation?

A brand purpose, mantra and core values review and definition is the best single activity you can do to address this challenge.

6. How can we monitor and protect the brand?

Several research tools are very important if you are serious about brand management as a process. These are:

- The Brand Strength Monitor, a large-scale quantitative survey that tracks the strength of the relationship between your brand, your customers and likely future prospects.
- The Brand Positioning Depth Workshop, two hour structured conversations with stimulus and projection exercises conducted with target consumers to explore your brand field and category territory.
- Social Media keyword listening tools to monitor and analyze the content

of online chatter about your brand.

- Brand Positioning Audits & Gap Analysis.
- Category context analysis and audits to evaluate what is and isn't being done in the category that could be done to take your brand position to a new level.
- The Brand Bible, which defines the visual and design standards for expressing the brand across all media channels and forms.
- Brand Essence Audit, which looks at the company's purpose, core values and essential principles for expressing your brand in a way that people on the outside can feel and relate to.

D | *The BrandSpark Workshop*

Successful brand storytellers focus the listener's minds on a single important idea, and it usually takes no longer than 30 seconds to forge an emotional connection. If a story concept is insightful and artistically rendered it can readily support the triple goal we've mentioned of boosting sales, strengthening the internal culture, and enhancing brand image.

But to arrive at a concept worthy of such a deep campaign requires research and introspection, leading to a brief that is then used to engage the talent of outside storytellers or advertising agencies that are engaged to work on your brand positioning challenge.

The BrandSpark workshop is a process to review the current business and brand situation and consider what kinds of additional work assignments your team needs to engage in to articulate your desired brand positioning.

In preparing the workshop there is a spectrum of brand planning topics to consider: What is a brand? What is brand planning? What is brand strength monitoring? What are the most cost effective methods for monitoring brand strength? What kinds of customer segmentation and profiling tools exist? Which ones might be the most helpful?

The graphic on the following page clusters these questions into topic areas that you can use to identify the most important themes for your own organization to address.

BRANDSPARK WORKSHOP PLANNING QUESTIONS

The Brand's Interactive Field ⇧ ⇩		Hidden beliefs, Values, Motivations, Relevance and Resonance linked to leverage lie in this field.

Company Questions	Key Findings	Differentiation	Strategy	CUSTOMERS
Brand Plan Process? Brand Guardians? Recent Brand Audit? Brand Gap Analysis? Brand Field Scan? Consumer Insights? Use of strong consumer insights methods?	Research Findings Research Methods?	The Brands Core Meaning? DNA Defined? Brand Personality? Brand Character? Resonance Achieved	Has Marketing & Branding been integrated?	Targeting Concerns? Any suspected Blindspots or Limiting Beliefs? Have customers ever been questioned to assess to energy impact of different elements of your marketing mix?
	SYNTHESIS OF ... Have research findings been translated into Brand Initiatives?	BRAND SPARK PLANNING	Tactics Coordinate marketing and branding activities	

Situation 1: Current State
Describe the current business & brand situation in terms of SWOT. Where do you question the value of products, programs, resources or alignment?

Situation 2: The Desired State
Describe your future brand positioning goals in detail. What do you want people in the future to believe about your products, company & brand?

E | *Soulful References & Case Studies*

1) Iron John by Robert Bly. Addison-Wesley Publishing 1990
In this deeply learned book, poet and translator Robert Bly offers nothing less than a new vision of what it is to be a man

2) The Seat of the Soul by Gary Zukav. Simon & Schuster, 1990
Zukav explains how we evolved from pursuing power based only upon the five senses into a species that pursues authentic power that is based upon values and spirit.

3) The Aquarian Conspiracy: Personal and Social Transformation in Our Time by Marilyn Ferguson, A Jeremy P. Tarcher/Putnam Book, 1980
From the early 1960s through the present day, many Americans have significantly changed their perspectives about the nature and purpose of work, relationships, religion, education, medicine, and indeed almost all public and private institutions. A great shift in values is taking place throughout the world, and this is the one book most closely identified with describing this movement's origins and underlying philosophy.

4) Subtle Energy: Awakening to the Unseen Forces In Our Lives by William Collinge, PhD, Warner Books, 1998
A noted teacher and researcher explains how we and our world are made of energy, and calls us to thoughtfully reconsider the inexplicable sensations and perceptions that we too easily dismiss. He then shows us how we can become attuned to those forces and harness their powers.

5) Care of the Soul by Thomas Moore, Harper-Collins Publishers, 1992
This book is considered to be one of the best primers for soul work. Thomas Moore, an internationally renowned theologian and former Catholic monk, offers a philosophy for living that involves accepting our humanity rather than struggling to transcend it. By nurturing the soul in everyday life, Moore shows how to cultivate dignity, peace, and depth of character.

6) The Re-Enchantment of Everyday Life by Thomas Moore, Harper-Collins Publishers, 1996

This book shows that a profound, enchanted engagement with life is not a childish thing to be put away with adulthood, but a necessity for our personal and collective survival.

7) Spirit Into Sound by Mickey Hart, Greatful Dead Books 1999

A compelling collection of quotes and reflections on the power of music.

8) Love and the Soul: Creating a Future For Earth by Robert Sardello, HarperPerennial 1996

This book proposes that inner work must be constantly balanced by a care for soul qualities in the world to avoid falling into egotism and self-absorption.

9) Creativity, Inc. Overcoming the Unseen Forces That Stand In The Way of True Inspiration, by Ed Catmull, Random House 2014

The insights in Soulful Branding regarding the human interactive field are validated in this far ranging narrative by the President of Pixar Animation and Disney Animation, which explains how Pixar achieved so many blockbuster movie successes. Perhaps one of the best business books ever written.

10) Catching the Big Fish by David Lynch, Jeremy P. Tarcher/Penguin, 2007.

Acclaimed filmmaker David Lynch provides a rare window into his methods as an artist, his way of capturing and working with ideas, and the immense creative benefits he has experienced that come with the practice of meditation.

11) The Chi Revolution by Bruce Frantzis, Energy Arts, 2008.

Timeless wisdom about tai chi, yoga, sex, aging, meditation and energetic fitness that will change the way you approach your health and spiritual practice.

F | *Deep Advertising Campaign Examples*

Deep Campaigns are different from other kinds of advertising campaigns in the following ways:

- They are linked to the purpose, mission and DNA of the company and brand.
- They speak as loudly to the people inside the company as they do to people on the outside.
- They are deeply linked to the character of the company and brand.
- They offer a solid positioning platform that can be interpreted in new ways over extended periods of time.
- They are often tied to soulful sensibilities and values, such as presenting messages that are inspirational, aspirational or uplifting.
- They often employee symbolism, music, arresting imagery and connect deeply to a brand's internal culture and soul.
- They aim to be salient, relevant and resonant at the same time, which is the sweet spot for breakthrough advertising.

Here are eight examples:

1) Nike: "Just Do It"

Just Do It was a campaign theme that tapped deeply into the ethos of the Nike brand. Trend research showed funding for school sports declining, and a rising obesity epidemic, and as Nike is a company of athletes, designing shoes and apparel for athletes Just Do It became the internal culture's call to action and allowed the brand to show inspirational scenes and moments across all sports for decades, building a stronger character association for the brand.

2) Apple: "Think Different"

Many advertising and marketing scholars cite Apple's 1984 as the most impactful Apple advertisement, but by our reckoning the major turning point in

Apple's brand rejuvenation came after Steve Jobs returned to Apple after being absent for ten years. Jobs knew the Apple brand had suffered from neglect, and that it needed to re-establish its core values and reconnect with the people it served in a meaningful way. The "Think Different" campaign accomplished all of these things simultaneously. (See Chapter 11 for a more detailed story about this remarkable campaign.)

3) Google: "Parisian Love"

The "Google 5," a handful of students recruited from ad and design schools, created this 2011 Super Bowl spot in-house. It presents the "life enhancing" role that Google search can play in bringing people together and assisting in travel and life planning. How people search for the things they need in life is pretty much at the core of the Google brand, and this campaign clearly links the core mission, values and DNA of the brand with how its services can make a tremendous difference in people's lives. The campaign was salient, relevant and emotionally resonant.

4) Facebook: "The Things That Connect Us"

This was an attempt at a deep campaign that didn't quite make it. It had almost all of the ingredients, but it missing several things. It was explanatory and descriptive (in a metaphorical way) of what Facebook is all about, but lacked emotional resonance (heart) and also lacked a strong connection with the purpose or mission of the brand.

5) BMW: "The Ultimate Driving Machine"

This campaign theme has been part of BMW's brand character since the 1970s. A recent TV ad says, "We don't make sports cars. We don't make SUVs. We don't make hybrids. We don't make luxury sedans. We only make one thing. The Ultimate Driving Machine." The precision craftsmanship, design and performance of BMW cars emanates from the center of the company's culture, and is well reinforced by the products and the advertising. Body, mind and spirit are tightly aligned and producing cohesive wave energy forms, consistently and over time. This brand character strongly supports BMW's position as the leading German automobile brand.

6) Starbucks: "Meet Me At Starbucks"

This was Starbucks first brand campaign, notable because the campaign is not focused on Starbucks products, but on the people who meet in its cafés, and on the kind of interactions that can only happen when people come face to face. These moments of human contact are at the very center of Starbucks brand character, and the campaign shows that Starbucks understands that it's in the people business first and the coffee business second, and that it is the soulful side of coffee and coffee moments that enables this kind of connection to be made. The purpose, mission and DNA of the brand are aligned with the spirit of the message.

7) FullSail University: "Real World Education in Entertainment Media Arts"

This university is the largest entertainment, media and arts college in the world. It has won several webby awards for its online storytelling and alignment of purpose, vision and brand DNA to communicate an inspirational message and an uplifting spirit, grounded in real world education. This school followed soulful branding principles and employed many of the tools and planning techniques presented here to help it achieve a vision of brand growth with integrity through integration of core values, mission, purpose, brand storytelling and entertaining approaches to present what they do and how they do it. The combined effect of the integrated values and storytelling has been rapid business growth since 2008.

8) University of Oregon – Masters in Sports Marketing Management.

This degree program at the University or Oregon was designed in close collaboration with the Sports Footwear and Apparel industry, and while the campaign to create awareness of the program is still largely under the radar for most people, it's worthy of mention here because the quality of its promotional video not only shows what the program teaches, but how it is integrated and embedded with the companies that employ its graduates. This level of integration in purpose, mission, DNA and story with the outside world is rare in the education field.

Acknowledgments

We are grateful to Doug Glen, who helped inspire this book and has given generously of his time and talents to read, comment and guide it to completion. We are also indebted in this regard to Po Chi Wu and Ian Bennett.

Our profound thanks to Scott Bedbury and Bill Barrett for all those intimate, caffeine fueled discussions about what is possible in a new brand world, to Tinker Hatfield for perspective and counsel on what is possible for a brand to do with design, to Tom Clarke and Mark Parker for being the patient, present processors of Nike's brand reality moment by moment during those 'Just Do It' years and still, miraculously today, to all the product line marketers and marketing directors at Nike 1986 – 1996 particularly the women's marketing team, Liz Dolan, Deborah Hilleren, Nancy Monsarrat, Darcy Winslow, Janet Champ, Ellen Schmidt Devlin, Kate Bednarski, Marla Murray, Juliet Moran, Chris Aveni, Hisako Esaki, Michelle Glaser Jackson, Ann Marie Lee, Ron Hill, Kirk Richardson, Peter Ruppe, Skip Lei, Mike Wilskey, Bob Wood, Tom Hartge, Claire Hamill, Chris Van Dyke, Bink Smith, Wilson Smith and Bill Worthington, all were solid marketing strategic partners and visionaries with both feet planted in thin air.

Thanks to Phil Knight for his support, providing a soulful internal atmosphere for exploration and risk taking that allowed all of us to take Nike's marketing and branding to the next level, finding better stories and always looking to make things tie.

Our appreciation also goes to Starbucks CEO Howard Schultz for challenging our retail design and marketing team to build a better brand, and to Wright Massey, Starbucks architect / visionary. Thank you Howard Behar for your sage, worldly perspective on Starbucks values and potential and Dave Olson and Mary Williams who knew how to stress and test the bean, to Arthur Rubenfield, Yves Mizrahi and George Murphy for their strategic guidance in the fastest retail store expansion in history.

Thanks to Deidre Wager, Christine Day and Nancy Kent for juggling many competing demands on the Starbucks brand, to Don Ohlmeyer at NBC who had the vision and courage to look outside the Primetime TV industry for a more insightful way to develop TV programming, to Quincy Jones for passionate and playful perspective into the role and power of music in global culture, particularly in movies and television, to Deepak Chopra for our many conversations about the nature of soul, to Tony Naughtin for his support and insight surrounding who and what runs the internet, to Jon Phelps, Ed Haddock, Bill Heavener, Gary Jones, Isis Jones, Ken Goldstone, Craig Daily, Nell Thompson and the rest of the team at FullSail for their courage and vision putting a soulful brand master planning process into play, to Tyrone Davis at Urban Icon for his passion and intense interest in branding heart and soul.

We've had the distinct privilege of working with a number of masters on many strategic research projects over the years, including Webb Green and Kathleen Byrne of TRD Frameworks Seattle. We are particularly indebted to British qualitative research pioneers Arnie Jacobsen, Vicky Johns, Lisa Grey, Val Smith and Roy Langmaid for their deep and enduring insights into the art of conducting depth workshops.

Thanks also to Steve Roth of Research International New York, Simon Wyld of BrainJuicer Los Angeles, Irma Zandl of the Zandl Group New York, Watts Wacker, the noted futurist and author and many in-house sharp research and marketing minds including Mike Franklin, Steve Phoutrides and Kevin King at Nike, Ed Clarke and Cherilyn Whalen Frei at Starbucks, Geoff Huntington, Ellen Yazejian, Lindy DeKoven and John Landgraf at NBC Entertainment, and Karen Hunt Simpson, Scott French and Bill Hankes at Internap.

And finally, we offer a special thanks to Gaya Blair Pendleton for creating a sense of order and structure out of our initial attempts to tell the story of soulful branding.

About the Authors

Jerome Conlon has thirty years brand development experience, including twenty in the strategy hot seat of several high profile world-class brands. He is a brand architect and a senior marketing executive who has unleashed triple-digit growth at a number of major brands, expanding their meaning, relevance and resonance to wider circles of consumers. He is a widely recognized leader in peak brand performance strategies by harnessing the power of brand intangibles.

Jerome is former Global Director of Brand and Marketing Insights for Nike, Inc., Vice President of Brand Planning, Consumer Insights and New Products for Starbucks Coffee Company, Senior VP of Marketing and Program Development for NBC Entertainment, and has guided dozens of other brands like FullSail University, on consulting engagements as president of Brand Frameworks and since 2014 as a principle consultant with FutureLab Innovation Consulting.

Moses Ma is the founder of a San Francisco venture incubator, Next-GEN ventures, was the inventor of Internet gaming, helped to establish XML as a business standard for the semantic web, and was a Fellow at the CommerceNet, Nokia Innovent and the Idea Factory think tanks. He is also the designer of the Agile Innovation Toolkit. Moses has contributed deep insights on the field of innovation and personal creativity, as well as the application of consciousness and mindfulness practices to business. He was also instrumental in helping to define a distinctly new and powerful process called ethography – the systematic study of a brand's character. Moses started out his career by inventing one of the world's first networked computer games, and along the way he has developed as a poet and artist, a filmmaker, and scientist. Having studied physics at Caltech, his insights were instrumental in developing the idea of the brand field.

Langdon Morris is CEO and co-founder of InnovationLabs, one of the world's leading innovation consultancies, and also co-founder of FutureLab, a unique strategy and technology firm. He works with leading organizations on all continents to help them develop and implement world class innovation tools, methods, and systems, and to help them attain success in a rapidly changing world. He is author or co-author of a dozen books on innovation and strategy that are read and studied worldwide.

Index

A

B

C

D

E

F

G

H

I

J

K

L

M

N

O

P

petroglyphs, 36
Pixar, 41, 192
Procter & Gamble, 7
psychographics, 123, 164
psychology, 7, 66, 78, 124

purpose, 21, 29-31, 39-42, 59, 63, 72, 79, 83, 89, 91-92, 95-96, 98-99, 101, 108, 114, 119-120, 130, 160-161, 164, 178, 182, 187-188, 191, 193-195
pyramid, 28, 167-169

Q

quantum theory, 24, 70, 72, 74, 86-89

R

relationships, 6, 19-20, 24, 26, 28, 32, 38, 64, 85, 88, 92, 99, 112, 124, 136, 145-146, 151, 157, 177, 191

Roddick, Anita, 133
Rodman, Dennis 143

S

Schultz, Howard, 22-23, 128, 196
Schumpeter, Joseph, 123, 156
Schwartz, Gary, 73
segmentation, 62, 182, 189
Senek, Simon, 99
soulfulness, 15, 17, 23-24, 28, 40, 145
soundscape, 36
Spengler, Oswald, 152
Spielberg, Steven, 37

Starbucks, 6, 9, 18-19, 22-23, 51, 60-61, 127-131, 160-161, 176, 178, 194-198
storytelling, 12, 21, 28, 31, 42, 47-48, 89, 102-104, 136-138, 154, 163, 166, 180, 184, 186-187, 195
strategy, 17, 32, 44, 46, 63, 66, 88, 97, 99, 112, 119-120, 138, 159, 162, 177
symbolism, 79, 93, 193
synthesis, 177, 190

T

teamwork, 13, 40, 49, 65, 78, 103, 146, 160
transformational, 5, 21, 57, 91

trustworthiness, 139-140

W

Weiden & Kennedy, 46

End Note

Branding at the deepest level is all about "soul". The soul is sensed with our "feelings" and with our "intuition." We experience soulful moments when we live into things that brighten our mood and cause our spirit to soar. Soulful moments usually occur when some deep truth is revealed to us. Soulfulness is a quality of subtle energy that we experience. People crave soulful experiences because this is when they "feel" most alive.

Every company and brand radiates with subtle energy that people intuitively sense. And if your brand is to become iconic and soulful you first need to identify the essence of the subtle energy that drives it. Then it is possible to emanate a kind of soulfulness that customers crave, to bring meaning or a feeling of more aliveness into their lives.

CPSIA information can be obtained
at www.ICGtesting.com
Printed in the USA
BVHW031934270821
615457BV00004B/79